Second Edition

Visual
Impact,
Visual
Teaching

Dedicated to "the inspiration"
and the vision of children throughout the world.

Second Edition

Visual Impact, Visual Teaching

Using Images to Strengthen Learning

Timothy Gangwer

CORWIN PRESS
A SAGE Company

For information:

Corwin Press
A SAGE Company
2455 Teller Road
Thousand Oaks, California 91320
www.corwinpress.com

SAGE India Pvt. Ltd.
B 1/I 1 Mohan Cooperative
   Industrial Area
Mathura Road, New Delhi 110 044
India

SAGE Ltd.
1 Oliver's Yard
55 City Road
London EC1Y 1SP
United Kingdom

SAGE Asia-Pacific Pte. Ltd.
33 Pekin Street #02-01
Far East Square
Singapore 048763

Printed in Singapore

Library of Congress Cataloging-in-Publication Data

Gangwer, Timothy.
Visual impact, visual teaching : using images to strengthen learning/Timothy Gangwer.
— 2nd ed.
      p. cm.
Includes bibliographical references and index.
ISBN 978-1-4129-6828-7 (cloth)
ISBN 978-1-4129-6829-4 (pbk.)
   1. Visual learning. 2. Learning, Psychology of. 3. Education—Audio-visual aids.
4. Thought and thinking. I. Title.

LB1067.5.G36 2009
370.15′23—dc22   2008031922

This book is printed on acid-free paper.

08   09   10   11   12   10   9   8   7   6   5   4   3   2   1

Acquisitions Editor:	Carol Chambers Collins
Associate Editor:	Megan Bedell
Editorial Assistant:	Brett Ory
Production Editor:	Amy Schroller
Copy Editor:	Alison Hope
Typesetter:	C&M Digitals (P) Ltd.
Proofreader:	Jeff Bryant
Indexer:	Judy Hunt
Cover Designer:	Karine Hovsepian

Contents

Foreword

As I ponder the role I am to assume as writer of the foreword to *Visual Impact, Visual Teaching*, I consider the numerous other roles I play in today's life. I ask myself, "Why pick me?" My most predominant characters have been illustrator and painter. I have no classroom or education experience.

You are likely a teacher—perhaps standing in a bookstore attempting to ascertain the value of this book by reading this foreword. What authority do I hold that would interest you in my opinion of the strategies? My career as an artist does center on visual communication. Professionally, I see the need for the next generation to have a vocabulary and skill for interpretation in place to understand and digest my work be it editorial illustration, book illustration or oil painting.

Or you could be a parent. AHA! There is a good connection. I am a father. As my boy speeds past the age of four, I have discovered that I have thoughts and, quite possibly, opinions on his future education. I also find that I have a desire to seek out information, opinions, and strategies so that I can feel confident in my actions and decisions concerning that education.

So my responsibility in today's role as "Foreword Writer" becomes clear— convince educators, parents, and more to read and utilize this book. Having found time to relax, read this book, and consider its meaning and usefulness, I'm inspired to make a contribution to its success in the education community. Go ahead. Read it and pass it on.

As my wife and I consider future schools, it is of high concern and importance to us whether or not the arts and art education are included in the curriculum. Unfortunately, such programs are limited and dwindling. "How is my son to develop the visual skills I so believe he needs? What about creative thinking and problem solving skills?" When the boy grows up and shuns my artistic ways in favor of being an attorney or an engineer, he'll need to be an adept creative thinker if he is to excel. He'll need to be able to decipher and understand the variety and abundance of visual stimuli that will surround him and influence him. He'll need to be prepared.

What I find great about the ideas set forth within this book is that the learning and concept exercises that would normally be accomplished in the art class might also be accomplished by the math teacher or the coach or even the principal or the parent. Also, no matter the knowledge content to be delivered, I recognize that an understanding of how to be a visual teacher would affect the performance of any educator and potentially greatly increase students' understanding and, most important, retention of information delivered. My son's future education looks better.

This book tells of how science has come a long way in understanding the way the brain works and how we as humans learn. I'm excited to learn here about the various learning styles that have been defined, the story behind the left brain/right brain concept, and just how many neurons fire in the blink of an eye. It is interesting to learn about how color and light affect the learning environment. This information provides some scientific authenticity to the strategies put forth. The strategies are then realized through a number of possible purposeful activities. My son's future education looks even better.

The activities and ways of carrying out classroom days as visual teachers seem fun and engaging. The elements of their implementation are simple and accessible. I'm even curious to perform the activities myself, to witness my own results. I recognize a similarity of the photo activity with my oil painting process. I know that when painting I don't approach a blank canvas with a specific notion in mind of what the end result will be. I begin simply making marks, which represent how I feel at that moment. Once the canvas is filled, I then turn it over and over until I find an image that I can make out if I use my imagination—like making out animals in clouds. I then apply painting skills to clarify the image. Much like the photo activity defined in this book, the end painting is very telling of my inner thoughts and feelings of the time when I created it. Why did I choose to make the face smiling? What am I expressing in that gesture? Why those clothes? Why red? The photo activity is such that it allows an unexpected tap into below-surface feelings, motivations, and perceptions. Tim clarifies the significance of this tap by relating his own inspiring experiences with the activity. These are great stories where understanding of the individual is achieved and the opportunity for learning is expanded—a success for both teacher and student.

My son is now four. It would be great to visit his kindergarten next year and witness the strategies of visual teaching being utilized and being successful. All it takes is to awake the creative spirit that dwells in each one of us. It is a valuable resource and aspect of being human. Good luck and good teaching.

—Nathan Jensen, Visual Artist
Austin, TX—www.natespace.com

Preface

Many people think verbally. The spoken language flows through the thought processes like a typewriter creating a story. All people think visually, continually translating words and ideas into pictures so that concepts and thoughts surface. In other words, we all understand, or decode, the visual language, but a true visual thinker has nonlinear thought, as if to be exercising cognition through computer simulation, then transforming the data into animation, or encoding. Thoughts become movies, images, and symbols. Language becomes multidimensional scenarios of concepts and ideas instead of the audible resonance of language. Ideally, the visual thinker has the ability to think beyond the meaning of language, using personal referents to meaning that cannot be translated into words. Visual thinking involves classification that is both parallel and holistic. Though linguistic thinkers may believe that visual thinkers center on detail, in fact this occurs because of the powerful memory of visual thinkers. They literally "see" the answers to problems. This is a tremendous advantage, enabling students to build entire information systems using their imaginations. If you would like to witness what happens in the mind of a visual thinker, look over their shoulder as they construct a jigsaw puzzle.

Bob Horn, a visiting researcher at Stanford University, believes visual language will change the world. He maintains that it is far more effective at conveying convoluted ideas than conventional methods of communication. The practice of visual thinking becomes a weapon against the "fire hoses of data" that threatens to overwhelm us in the twenty-first century. Visual language has its own formal rules of syntax and semantics. These have been subliminally etched in our thinking from years of visual media, particularly through the ten techniques of persuasive advertising: Humor, Macho, Friends, Family, Fun, Nature, Sexy, Cartoon, Celebrity, and Wealth. Every day someone is "renting your eyeballs."

There are very rigid rules in the syntax of the written or spoken language. For example, "What time it is?" is understandable, but incorrect.

The visual language rules are far more casual, since the visual language summons the unique, creative, internal-visual diction of its user. Consider the power of integrating the spoken or written language with the visual language. I can tell young children over and over how to tie their shoes and they may never learn. However, if I model the act while describing the process, in little or no time at all every child will master the art and it will very quickly become second nature. Because the brain processes verbal and visual information in different pathways, these children receive the information in two forms, forcing them to use more of the brain.

Visual learning is not new. From the Paleolithic cave paintings, to the Egyptian hieroglyphics, to the visual language used in our modern-day world, we have always been a visual society. The visual language remains an important component of our evolution, which begs the question "Is the visual language an important component of our educational strategies?" *Visual Impact, Visual Teaching* is written to expose educators, administrators, and parents to the framework that defines the visual teacher by highlighting the methodology and research to areas such as visual learning and critical visual thinking. The intent of this book is to give the reader a sense of where we've been, where we are, and where we need to be in our learning environments.

In the twenty-first century, we know so much more about how the human brain functions. The brain-compatible learning approach outlined in this book aims to open the gateway to such important areas as differentiating instruction, multiple intelligences, character education, and lateral thinking skills. Readers will be armed with the visual communication tools necessary to encode and decode the visual language, while given knowledge of the applications of graphic organizers and glyphs.

Technology is the cause of one of the largest paradigm shifts in the world; our students are coming of age as the fabric of this shift cloaks their everyday lifestyle. That is why it is essential for educators to embrace technology-based instruction, using the Internet as a learning tool, and media literacy instruction.

There is much research on how fine arts are often the pivot point of instruction. It is difficult to teach any subject without including art. You will learn new ideas, such as the unique Watergraph process. When the budgetary axe falls, it is often the fine arts programs that are lost, thereby passing the instructional torch to the individual teacher. The visual strategies in this book are directed at those teachers, and at fine arts teachers as well.

With each passing day, the United States is becoming the example of a global community. Our educational system strives to meet the needs of the many English language learners through many effective programs and instructional modifications. Understanding the visual language is an effective universal language, this book emphasizes its importance by guiding students through a visual process, which ultimately translates to the comprehension and use of the oral and written language.

Visual Impact, Visual Teaching walks the reader along the path of becoming a visual teacher. Having reached the end of that path, you will find hundreds of practical, ready-to-use, subject-specific, multilevel visual-learning activities, all of which are designed to reinforce the information set forth throughout the book's entirety. The purpose of this book is to complement existing teaching styles and, quite literally, to change the way we perceive our world. Once the mind's eye has its opportunity to decipher information, the brain is able more easily to put that information in sync with spoken or written information. What takes place is a permanent change in the students' awareness and understanding. When our students' minds begin to change, so too does their ability to change the world.

Acknowledgments

Corwin Press gratefully acknowledges the contributions of the following reviewers:

Lydia Aranda, Elementary Teacher
San Antonio, TX

Laura S. Gulledge, Media Literacy Teacher
Benjamin Russell High School, Alexander City, AL

Ellen Herbert, Art Teacher
Longview High School, Longview, TX

Jude Huntz, Former Sixth-Grade English Teacher/Current Adult
  Education Coordinator
St. Michael the Archangel Catholic Parish, Leawood, KS

David Hyerle, Codirector
Designs for Thinking, Lyme, NH

Loukea Kovanis-Wilson, Chemistry Teacher
Clarkston High School, Clarkston, MI

Rhonda S. Robinson, Professor of Educational Technology, Research
  and Assessment
Northern Illinois University, DeKalb, IL

Diane Senk, ELL Teacher
Pigeon River Elementary School, Sheboygan, WI

Mary Turner
Northern Illinois University, DeKalb, IL

About the Author

 **Timothy Gangwer,** MA, is a pioneer in the field of visual learning and a dedicated educator of twenty-six years. He has served as Visual Literacy Consultant to the Ministry of Education, Paris, France; Ministry of Education, Toranomon, Japan; Mediterranean Association of International Schools, Casablanca, Morocco; Association of International Schools in Africa, Abidjan, Côte d'Ivoire; and as a trainer for the United States Department of Education's National Diffusion Network. He is an international keynote speaker, educational consultant, and the director and cofounder of the Visual Teaching Alliance. A former teacher of elementary-level students with learning disabilities, he is also an award-winning digital artist and songwriter. For information on professional development and on-site training seminars, contact the author at VTAlliance@aol.com or visit his Web site at www.VisualTeachingAlliance.com.

Other Books by Timothy Gangwer

From Both Sides of the Desk: The Best Teacher I Never Had

American Holidaze

English Works in America—EL Civics & ESL: Visual Communication Tools for Teachers (with Gloria Rzadko-Henry)

Picturing Our World (with Tom Crockett)

Science & Imagery (with Tom Crockett)

Holiday Handbook: A Year of Visual Learning Activities

1 What Is Visual Teaching?

During a rehearsal of Debussy's *La Mer,* Maestro Arturo Toscanini found himself unable to describe to the orchestra the effect he hoped to achieve from a particular passage. After a moment's thought, he took a silk handkerchief from his pocket and tossed it high into the air. The musicians, mesmerized, watched the slow, graceful descent of the silken square. Toscanini smiled with satisfaction as it finally settled on the floor. "There," he said. "Play it like that" (Fadiman, 1985).

This vignette is a perfect example of why this book is necessary. As a global community, we are in the midst of a paradigm shift. We are moving from a period in which the language of production and manufacturing dominated our way of seeing the world; now, ideas about information and communication shape our discourse. Could it be that we are actually in the midst of an even deeper change—one in which the pendulum of worldview is swinging from a more masculine and word-based culture to one that is more feminine and image based?

It is hard to ignore that the generation of children now moving through our educational system is by far the most visually stimulated generation that system has ever had to teach. Having grown up with cable television, video games, computer software that educates and entertains, and the Internet, our children are truly visual learners coming of age in an increasingly visually oriented world. Notwithstanding individual differences in intelligence and learning style, this generation of children needs to be taught the way they learn best—with visual stimulation accompanied by active learning strategies. As educators, we need to prepare our students for the world in which they will live and work. We must allow this understanding of the visual nature of our students to influence our teaching techniques and the educational technologies we employ. We need to become visual teachers.

INTRODUCTION TO VISUAL TEACHING

Whether you are an early childhood teacher or high school chemistry teacher, visual teaching is a template for all your instructional strategies.

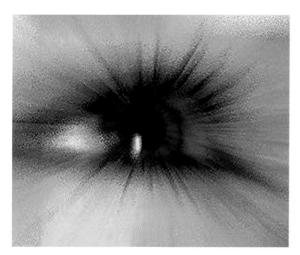

Since vision develops rapidly in the infant and so governs human sensory occurrence, it soon evolves into the dominant means through which children learn about their world. Our student population is made up of 65 percent visual learners, 30 percent auditory learners, and 5 percent kinesthetic learners (Mind Tools, 1998). Based on the concept that visual images are a language, visual literacy can be defined as the ability to understand and create visual messages. Development in the area of visual literacy has focused on the growth and expansion of educational programs that stimulate students' abilities to assess and produce a visual language, as well as enhancement of students' reading and writing skills through the use of visual literacy strategies.

> Visual Literacy refers to a group of vision-competencies a human being can develop by seeing and at the same time having and integrating other sensory experiences. The development of these competencies is fundamental to normal human learning. When developed, they enable a visually literate person to discriminate and interpret the visible actions, objects, symbols, natural or man-made, that he encounters in his environment. Through the creative use of these competencies, he is able to communicate with others. Through the appreciative use of these competencies, he is able to comprehend and enjoy the masterworks of visual communication.
>
> —(John Debes, cofounder of the International Visual Literacy Association, 1969, 27)

Visual literacy in the classroom has become increasingly important as more and more information and entertainment is accessed through technology. Students must maintain the ability to think critically and visually about the images presented to them in today's society. The Dale Cone of Experience model is based on the concept that learning evolves from the concrete to the abstract; visual symbols are nonverbal representations that precede verbal symbols (Sinatra, 1986). Because pictures or illustrations are analogs of experience and are only one step removed from actual events, these visual representations may be able to capture and communicate the concrete experience in various ways.

To address the effective use of visual skills in the pursuit of learning, visual learning theory has evolved into four key elements: full-spectrum visual learning, active and performance-based learning, dynamic translation, and a multidisciplinary approach.

> Although we should attempt to preserve textual notions of literacy, it would be a breach of our duties as teachers for us to ignore the rhetorical power of visual displays. Visual forms of media, by themselves, and in combination with text and sound, come at our students from all directions, including television and the World Wide Web. The critical media literacy we need to teach must include evaluation of these media, lest our students fail to see, understand, and learn to harness the persuasive power of visual media.
>
> —(Michael Day, Chair of the National Council of Teachers of English's Assembly for Computers in English (Day 1997)

Full-spectrum visual literacy is defined as the ability to understand nonlinguistic communication made with visual imagery and the ability to use visual imagery to communicate. Individuals become visually literate by means of the practices of visual encoding (expressing thoughts and ideas in visual form) and visual decoding (translating the content and meaning of visual imagery).

Active and performance-based learning is an active approach to engaging the world. Photography is an ideal medium for experiencing and encountering. People must constantly be challenged to apply knowledge to new and authentic situations as they use the tool of photography to interface with the real world.

Dynamic translation is the process of expressing ideas in new forms. When people take a thought and express it as an image, or object, or text presentation, they understand that thought in a deeper sense. Real learning has occurred when individuals can express ideas not simply in the form in which they were

originally delivered, but also in new and varied forms.

The multidisciplinary approach encourages writing and connecting, clustering and creative expression, imaging and visual thinking. This approach also reflects an awareness of the dynamics of various styles and modalities of learning and experience.

Visual skills can be learned. They are not usually isolated from other sensory skills. Teachers should provide appropriate learning environments and materials to allow students to create their own visual messages. Digital literacies such as computers, audiovisual materials, and multimedia, require different skills. Competency in one literacy does not necessarily transfer to another. Because visual arts can impact student emotions and assist in comprehension, teachers should guide students through the process of learning to recognize and respond to visual and print messages of humor, irony,

and metaphor. They may also require guidance to distinguish between factual and fictional visual representations. Students' learning rates increase when teachers support a variety of learning styles. Studies have shown that processing in reading and math involves both phonological and visual information, thereby increasing reading, writing, and mathematical skills through the use of visual literacy (Stix, 1996). In a study conducted with groups of students enrolled in a mathematics methods course (a required course using pictorial journals for those teaching at the elementary level), the groups reported a better sense of task and a more focused introduction to their visual learning journal. Both groups agreed that their math anxiety decreased and their self-confidence increased as a result of the pictorial journal assignments (Stix). If visual literacy is perceived as a language, then there is a need to know how to communicate using this language, which includes being attentive to visual messages and critically reading or viewing images as the language of the messages. Visual literacy, like language literacy, is culturally specific, although there are certainly universal symbols or visual images that are globally understood. "When words and visual elements are closely entwined, we create something new and we augment our communal intelligence . . . visual language has the potential for increasing 'human bandwidth'—the capacity to take in, comprehend, and more efficiently synthesize large amounts of new information" (Horn, 2001).

Who Is the Visual Teacher?

The visual teacher is an educator who

- embraces and models full-spectrum visual literacy and
- understands the effects of visual stimulation on brain development and, where appropriate, utilizes imagery to enhance learning.

The visual teacher understands

- the underlying concepts of visual literacy. Imagery communicates in an emotional and prerational style that can bypass logical thought. Imagery invokes the part of our brain that assembles symbols and visual elements into stories.

The visual teacher actively encourages

- students to decode still images, such as documentary or advertising photography; and
- moving images, such as commercials, newscasts, and dramatic or comic television programs and films.

The visual teacher explores

- with students the signs and symbols in art and visual media.

The visual teacher encourages

- students to encode or make more effective still images through an understanding of passive, neutral, and active imagery.

The visual teacher avoids

- passive learning experiences by bridging "seeing" and "doing" through the use of appropriate projects, activities, and technologies.

The visual teacher creates lesson plans and activities that reflect the methods of visual learning, acknowledging that when we create and utilize images we will most likely be working in one (or more) of the following modes:

- Investigate
- Communicate
- Chronicle
- Inspire
- Express
- Envision

The visual teacher responds to student image making, evaluating effectiveness based on criteria that correspond to the methods of visual learning:

- Did you discover something new (external)?
- Did you record your observation faithfully and accurately?
- Did you manifest an idea, thought, or feeling in visual form?
- Would a viewer "get" the idea, thought, or feeling you have expressed in visual form?
- Has your image changed a viewer's mind or influenced his or her behavior?
- Did you discover something new (internal)?

The visual teacher creates assignments and activities that allow students to develop and apply their visual information handling skills by using the abilities

- to organize images for effective display;
- to establish visual criteria and arrange images in a visual database;
- to substitute images for words and establish a visual language;
- to combine images with text to share ideas more effectively;
- to integrate images with live presentations to communicate more powerfully; and
- to alter, manipulate, or transform existing images to envision something new.

THE SIX METHODS OF VISUAL LEARNING

The visual teaching template is appropriate for all subjects and grade levels. Think of these methods in comparison to a computer. The computer can be used at any level or subject, simply by varying the software. Although the lessons of visual learning may vary, the six methods of visual learning are constant. Although imagery comes in all forms and varying media, a camera is an excellent classroom tool to enhance visual awareness and increase visual learning skills. Students naturally and honestly communicate through the lens of a camera. Their world of nonwritten, nonverbal communication is funneled through a small window. Instant cameras are particularly useful for classroom activities. They provide a tangible, instant product of the students' success, and images can immediately be integrated into the lesson.

Whether we choose a camera or pen, we are probably going to use that tool to investigate, chronicle, express, communicate, inspire, or envision. Each of these methods, whether we are writing or taking photographs, has its own set of expectations and criteria for evaluation. Understanding these methods will help you think about the types of assignments you give and the best way to understand the results.

1. Investigate

Seeing through the eye of a camera's viewfinder can often help focus attention and clarify thought. Investigating assignments ask participants to use words and images to learn about and better understand the world. Clustering, listing, visual-thinking maps, and other prewriting activities are examples of explorational methods of communication. Use the camera as a tool to observe, study, identify, and learn. As a tool for investigation, photography helps us focus our attention and concentrate on detail.

2. Chronicle

Chronicling assignments freeze moments in time. Documentary imagery and descriptive writing are examples of working in the chronicle method. We judge images by how honest or accurate they are. As a tool for documentation, imagery helps us record and annotate a rapidly changing world.

3. Express

Expressive works reveal thoughts and feelings and translate the abstract to the concrete. Visual journals and stream-of-consciousness techniques are expressive exercises. Use the camera to create a visual language and release your feelings into the world. Expressing activities help us bring our thoughts and emotions into a visual form. As a tool for expression, imagery gives us a glimpse of the world through the eyes of others.

4. Communicate

Assignments in communication are designed to share information with others. Formal elements such as structure, composition, and organization are essential when communicating. Visual reports and photojournalism are examples of methods of communication. How much information is being communicated? Is the information high quality? Is it clearly presented? As a tool for communication, imagery gives us a rich new language for sharing our ideas.

5. Inspire

Inspirational assignments use the power of communication to change behavior or attitude. Use images to influence others through the persuasive capability of photography. As a tool for inspiration, photography provides products of success and positive reinforcement.

6. Envision

Envisioning assignments encourage new connections and relationships. This communication helps establish both occupational and personal visual goals. Use the power of your imagination to envision something new. As a tool for creativity, photography puts the "image" back in "imagination." After all, imagination is a word taken from the Latin *imaginari,* which means, "to picture mentally" (American Heritage Dictionary, 1989).

Eighteen Tips for the Visual Teacher

1. Challenge the roles of the teacher, learner, and community as creative thinkers, designers, and innovators.

2. Teach character education, problem solving, and critical thinking skills; practice cooperative learning.

3. Remember that educators are choreographers and facilitators of the learning process.

4. Remember that the tools of multimedia technology are essential elements of academic success.

5. Believe in the integration of fine arts in all subject matter and at every level.

6. Integrate brain-compatible strategies and mind-mapping techniques in your lessons and teaching strategies.

7. Be an interdisciplinary teacher and utilize differentiated instructional approaches.

8. Remember that hands-on and eyes-on experiences, resources, and networking strategies are tools of empowerment.

9. Allow your students to influence your teaching techniques and the educational technologies you employ.

10. Use visual aids such as imagery and computer presentations.

11. Anything a student can see and manipulate promotes hands-on and eyes-on teaching.

12. During reading instruction, do not isolate phonetics. Be sure to emphasize the sight approach.

13. Practice configuration during spelling instruction. For example, if you draw a line around the letters in the word "bed," you will find the line takes on the shape of an actual bed.

14. Try to avoid rote memorization. Exercise conceptual and inductive strategies.

15. Stress creativity, critical visual thinking, and exercise of the imagination, as opposed to a focus on facts alone.

16. Encourage students to sketch visual representations of what is being taught. This is not about being an artist—it is about exercising visual translation.

17. Use computers! Technology is not a fad. The best time to purchase a new computer is today!

18. Above all, keep in mind, "The future of teaching has arrived."

Subject-Specific Suggestions

Mathematics

- Color-code math problems.
- Use graph paper to arrange math problems.
- Use visual cues such as manipulatives and flashcards.

Spelling and Writing

- Outline words with colored marking pens.
- Create a visual image of the word before writing it.
- Use visual study aids rather than recitation.

Reading

- Visualize vocabulary by looking at the word, closing your eyes, then recreating it in the mind's eye.
- Look up the definition of new vocabulary words so they can be seen in a different context.
- Use graphs, flow charts, visual thinking maps, visual image mapping, and visual links.

Science and Social Studies

- Use colored pens to take notes, following this pattern: main themes = red; supporting details = blue; specific details = green.
- When introducing new material, use visual simulations such as video, computers, and role-play.

CRITICAL VISUAL THINKING

When children enter the educational system, typically they go through some standard form of screening, which generally takes twenty minutes or less for each child. The screening protocol usually looks at these areas:

- drawing and copying: hand preference, approach to task, comfort level, and fine motor skills (grip)
- remembering: visual and auditory, remembering what is seen and heard
- building with blocks: perception, fine motor skills (dexterity), and eye-hand coordination
- using language: to describe and to reason
- coordinating body movements: balancing, hopping, and skipping

Unless specific problems arise during the screening, it is assumed the child is ready to learn. After the kindergarten curriculum is covered, the child moves to the first grade and repeats this gradual yearly process until the student has completed the twelfth grade. The most critical mistake in our educational system is that we never teach the students how to learn. Instead, we only teach them what to learn. By teaching them how to learn, we help them develop critical visual thinking skills. Students come without training in those skills, while teachers tend instinctively to take the presence of those skills for granted. Yet without critical visual thinking structurally integrated into instruction, learning may be temporary and perfunctory.

Critical visual thinking is the identification and evaluation of visual evidence, thinking in pictures, creating imagery in the mind's eye, and the ability to formulate that imagery into a visual language to guide decision-making. Critical visual thinking involves logical thinking and reasoning, including skills such as comparison, classification, sequencing, cause and effect, patterning, webbing, analogies, deductive and inductive reasoning, forecasting, planning, hypothesizing, and critiquing. It involves creating something new or original. It involves the skills of flexibility, originality, fluency, elaboration, brainstorming, modification, imagery, associative thinking, attribute listing, metaphorical thinking, and forced relationships. The aim of critical visual thinking is to stimulate curiosity and promote divergence. It is divided into six psychological guidelines: lucidity, veracity, purpose, intensity, dimension, and coherence.

Guideline I. Lucidity

Students seek elaboration, examples, and illustrations of meaning. Take, for instance, the question, "What can we do about global warming?" A critical visual thinker would deem this question unclear. An explicit alternative to the question would be, "What can humans do to establish individual goals and task forces to begin an immediate implementation of the mandated steps needed in the fight against global warming?"

Guideline II. Veracity

Students question the truthfulness of the information and request paths to follow to check personally on its validity. "When it rains, the sidewalks will get wet." Critical visual thinkers would initially regard this statement to be true by using inductive reasoning. They envision the last time it rained and visualize wet sidewalks. However, the veracity guideline requires the addition of deductive reasoning. For instance, visualize an awning built over the sidewalk since the last time it rained, or visualize two people standing side-by-side on the sidewalk, each holding a large umbrella.

Guideline III. Purpose

Students question the relevance of the information, and seek a solid connection to the question at hand. "When two laborers work the same number of hours, they should receive the same amount of pay." A critical visual thinking would question the relevance of the hours spent working and visualize the amount of productivity between the workers.

Guideline IV. Intensity

Students magnify the information for its complexities, while continuing to examine its relevance. An example is the statement, "He's a good guy." A critical visual thinker would want the word "good" defined. The statement may be accurate, but it is vague. Is he a good guy because he has not broken the law? Compared to whom is he a good guy? This guideline requires a deeper probe into the information.

Guideline V. Dimension

Students begin to shift focus to alternative viewpoints. "Democrats are more productive than Republicans." Although this statement is concise, the critical visual thinker would not find it insightful and would look at all issues in both political parties that would make the statement true or false.

Guideline VI. Coherence

Students track their thinking and create a visual flowchart ensuring that there is a definitive beginning, middle, and end. The critical visual thinker would look for sensible sequence, thereby deeming the information logical. However, any trace of ambiguity or contradictions would illustrate that the piece of information is illogical, overall.

The ideal critical visual thinker is always curious, well-informed, confident, flexible, virtuous in facing personal biases, sensible in making judgments, willing to reexamine, explicit about issues, orderly in complex matters, assiduous in seeking pertinent information, reasonable in the selection of criteria, inquisitive, and determined to seek consequences that are as accurate as the subject and the conditions of inquiry permit.

Socratic Teaching

One of the oldest and perhaps the most robust teaching methods for cultivating any form of critical thinking is known as Socratic teaching. In Socratic teaching, the focus is on questions, not answers. We lead from behind, and the truth is discovered, not delivered. As a strategy, Socratic questioning is a highly disciplined process. The Socratic teacher acts as the cogent equal of the inner critical voice that the mind and mind's eye create when the inner critical voice generates critical thinking abilities. The input from the students is like thoughts in the mind. All of the thoughts are addressed carefully and fairly. By pursuing all answers with questions, and by selecting questions that promote discussion and debate, the Socratic teacher guides the students to think in a regulated, intellectually responsible fashion, while assisting the students by asking additional questions.

The Socratic teacher ensures that

- students are in a continuous dialogue with the teacher;
- learning is constructed, not fed;
- the teacher is functioning as a facilitator or mentor, and not as a lecturer; and
- questions are answered with explanations or further questions, and not simply with "yes" or "no."

Evidence of a Socratic teacher

- Pertinent discussions on related issues often break out.
- Debate is common.
- Peers exchange ideas.
- Student and teacher satisfaction increases.
- "Rabbit chasing" becomes an art—exploring related issues while remaining on task.
- Teachers often face questions for which they have no answers.
- Social interaction and peer acceptance in the class is generally high.
- Objectives, activities, and assessments are tied to higher-level behavioral verbs.
- All students have the opportunity to interact with the teacher and peers.
- Time in the lesson is allowed for debating.
- Socratic teachers encourage both inductive and deductive reasoning.

REINFORCING CRITICAL VISUAL THINKING SKILLS

Once critical visual thinking skills have been introduced, students must exercise them within the context of daily lessons. Through time, these skills will become habitual and will become the foundation of thought. There are three excellent methods that can be easily integrated into the existing curricula: the TPCASTT Poem Analysis Method, deBono's Six Thinking Hats, and the game of chess.

TPCASTT

TPCASTT is an acrostic for **T**itle **P**araphrase **C**onnotation **A**ttitude **S**hifts **T**itle **T**heme. Using TPCASTT, any poem, regardless of length or intellectual level, can be used to guide students.

Title. Suggest that the students think about the title before reading the poem. Probe the students' opinions, and remind them that there are no incorrect answers. In E. E. Cummings's poem, "If Strangers Meet," the title may imply what will happen when two people who have never met come together. However, the word "if" could imply that there remains the possibility that these two strangers may never meet.

Paraphrase. Ask the students to translate the poem into their own words. Again, it is important the students understand there are no incorrect answers. After each student reads the paraphrased poem, each should give examples of personal experiences that relate to what is happening in the poem.

Connotation. Encourage the students to contemplate the poem for meaning beyond the literal. Although they denied having done so, songwriters John Lennon and Paul McCartney were repeatedly asked whether the title of the song "Lucy in the Sky With Diamonds" was an acrostic for the psychedelic drug LSD.

Attitude. How does the poet feel about the poem? Encourage students to put themselves in the shoes of the poet. What was the inspiration? Was Cummings seated at a park bench and joined by a passing stranger? Was he seated on a bus watching two strangers conversing? Did he see a man run to a taxi, only to watch it drive away?

Shifts. Help students take note of transitions in the poem. Tell them that the shifts and transitions in a poem are with purpose. In Cummings's poem, the first three lines could easily have been the opening line, yet he specifically chose to divide it into three.

Title. Have the students examine the title again, this time on an interpretive level, to examine their findings. Did their initial speculation of the title's meaning meet their expectations, or did the content of the poem alter the title's meaning for them?

Theme. Together, determine what the poet thinks about the subject. Explore the poet's mood during the inspiration and writing period. Since the poet is not present, speculation is encouraged. You may wish to instigate discussion and debate with statements such as, "I think the poet was very angry when he wrote this poem," or "I think the poet didn't intend for anyone ever to read this poem."

de Bono's Six Thinking Hats

Edward de Bono is regarded by many to be the leading expert in the field of creative thinking and the direct teaching of thinking as a skill. He introduced the concept of lateral thinking, which treats creativity as the action of information in a self-organizing information system—such as the neural systems in the brain. de Bono's "Six Thinking Hats" technique enables a person to look at significant decisions from various different perspectives. It assists in better decision making by forcing the decision maker to move outside the typical thinking pattern. It helps a person understand the full intricacy of the decision, and depicts matters and opportunities that you might otherwise have overlooked.

Each thinking hat represents a different style of thought, and each represents an excellent way to reinforce critical visual thinking. By placing six colored hats in the front of the classroom, at any given moment you can stop a lesson, discussion, or debate, and ask a student, "Based on the comment you just made, which of these hats were you wearing?" This brings thinking to a visual level. The hats are visual, tangible, and a constant marker of the critical visual thinking process.

White Hat: Knowledge. Look at the information you have and see what you might learn from it.

- Who? What? When? Where? How? Why?
- What do you know about . . . ?
- What are the facts about . . . ?
- What do you need or want to know about . . . ?
- Where might you go to find out about . . . ?

Red Hat: Evaluation of Feelings. Look at the information through intuition and emotion.

- What are your feelings now?
- Did your feelings change?

- What prejudices are present?
- What does your intuition tell you?

Black Hat: Analysis. Look at the information carefully and defensively.

- What should you be cautious about?
- What words of wisdom come from this?
- What are the consequences of . . . ?
- What were the difficulties of . . . ?
- What are the risks of . . . ?

Yellow Hat: Positives. Look at the information optimistically.

- What are the benefits of . . . ?
- What is a positive outcome of . . . ?
- Can this be made to work? Explain.
- What did you like about . . . ?

Green Hat: Creative Ideas. Look at the information with freewheeling thinking.

- What if . . . ?
- Can you create other ways to do this?
- How would you solve the problem?
- Express yourself through literature, poetry, media, and the Meisner technique (role-play and drama).

Blue Hat: Understanding. Look at the information with comprehension, confidence, and autonomy.

- Sequence your events.
- Summarize.
- Articulate your conclusion.
- Articulate your action plan
- Define the problem, and how it was solved.
- Track your thinking.

Chess

James Santorelli, associate director of the National Scholastic Chess Foundation and a chess teacher in several White Plains, New York, schools, said, "With chess, children can practice deductive reasoning and use it in day-to-day situations. The idea with increasing the number of curricular programs is to improve children's critical thinking skills and analytical abilities" (Merri Rosenberg, "Playing Chess as a Tool in Learning," *New York Times*, October 11, 1992). Chess is a game of visual problem solving and taps into higher-level thinking skills. Students that often have difficulty recalling details from a passage of text typically do not experience problems with recalling chess moves. They are recalling pieces of visual representations in which particular configurations are recognized. These associate with, and often prompt, previous successful responses or pattern responses. It is a game of divergent thinking requiring students to think several moves ahead, which is an excellent method of exercising critical visual thinking skills. Chess challenges students in logic and deductive reasoning. It is also a game of socialization where students teach each other with visual decisions. They are taught how to think, and not what to think. They must constantly shift their thinking and reasoning, while being creative in their strategy.

Other benefits of chess include these:

- Chess instills in young students a sense of self-confidence and self-worth.
- Chess improves rational thinking.
- Chess increases cognitive skills.
- Chess improves communication skills and proficiency in recognizing patterns.
- Chess teaches the value of hard work and commitment.
- Chess teaches students they must be accountable for all actions and bear the consequences.

THE POWER OF VISUAL LEARNING

As teachers, we are constantly in search of that one modality we can best plug in to. Some students are auditory learners, others are tactile, and most are visual learners. Approximately 65 percent of all people are visual learners who relate most effectively to written information, notes, diagrams, and pictures (Kranzler, 1999). The challenge is to find the best approach in identifying that strength, then finding many ways to tap into it.

What are common characteristics of visual learners? Although not necessarily indicative of all visual learners, many recall specific directions after going to a location only once. They tend to like multifarious ideas and assignments and do well on them, yet often fail at simple things. Emotionally, they can be very sensitive and often have poor listening skills, or appear to be not listening. Most visual learners like art and music and are easily distractible. They may experience difficulty with multiplication tables and spelling, yet they love crossword puzzles, jigsaw puzzles, blocks, television, computers, and video games. This is due to the visual aids accompanied with these activities (i.e., crossword puzzles comprise letter blocks, or visual cues, commonly known as configuration). It is not uncommon for visual learning students to have difficulty completing assignments, and they can be overly sensitive to criticism. If you encounter students who are physically sensitive, and who often have heightened hearing and intense reactions to loud noises, they may be visual learners. They often have poor sense of time and appear disorganized. Their vivid imaginations can also lead to disturbing dreams.

There are lots of ideas that are easily implemented to support your visual learners. Allow them a clear view of you, their teacher, when you are speaking so they can see your body language and facial expressions. Encourage them to use color to highlight important points in text. Ask them to illustrate their ideas as a picture and use visual thinking maps. Make time for use of multimedia such as computers or videos. Create an area for them to study in a quiet place away from verbal disturbances. Understand that they will visualize information as a picture to aid their learning. Encourage making charts, graphs, and tables in their notes as study aids. Motivate them to participate actively in class, as it will keep them involved and alert. If you request that they memorize material, have them write it over and over, thereby engraving the visual image of text in their visual filing system.

Visual learning is often the strength behind the success of the student. Using photography as a tool to enhance this strength is a wonderful way to captivate and motivate these students. Photography is a universal language. Students naturally and honestly communicate with photographs. They do not know the rules—and in this case, not knowing the rules is a good thing. When you or I shoot a photo, we first check to ensure the sun is behind us and not in front of our lens. We then ask our subject to avoid standing in front of any brightly lit areas to avoid underexposure. When we have multiple subjects, we ask them to arrange themselves in a way that is cosmetically pleasing to our eye. The final request is to ask them to look at the camera, smile, and call out names of dairy products. All of this takes precedence over the language of photography. This is simply not true with students, because they do not know the rules. They take it as they see it. I believe this notion really speaks for children in general.

My youngest son, Casey, was on his way to preschool one morning. He announced, "Daddy, I want all my friends at school to know who my daddy is." I was pleased to know that I was finally allowed to escort Mr. Independent to his classroom—that is, until he informed me he would simply take my picture. I handed him an instant camera. He snapped a single shot and promptly placed it in his shirt pocket. On the way to school, he removed the photo from his pocket, smiled, and exclaimed, "Hey, Daddy, look! My picture turned out perfect!" Upon examination, I was surprised to find a photo taken of me from the belt buckle down. Now, being the encouraging father that I am, I complimented him on a job well done. On the drive home, I thought that if I had taken that photo, I would have disposed of it and shot another one. After all, I cut off the most important feature of my subject. And yet Casey felt it was perfect. Why? When I thought about it, I realized that because he only stood as tall as my belt buckle, unless he looked up or I squatted down, everything from my belt buckle down *is* Daddy to him.

Learn to appreciate the natural honesty that comes from a student's photographic communication. Students learn many wonderful things through the communicative exploration of imagery. As teachers, we often marvel at what students reveal when they communicate with symbols and images, even when they do not fully realize that they are communicating at all. Give a student a camera and ask him or her to take a photograph of a specific object. Technically, you have just asked that student to communicate nonverbally, without written expression. You have asked the student to communicate a collection of thoughts and translate ideas using nothing more than a photograph. Think of what you can learn from your students that you might otherwise miss—things you will not find in a permanent record, portfolio, psychoeducational battery of tests, or parent surveys.

In the fall of 1984, I was teaching a group of elementary students who had learning disabilities. One student was named James. He was a well-groomed young man, captain of his soccer team, and a leader among his peers. James appeared to have everything in the world going for him.

It was the last week of October, and Halloween was on the approaching Saturday. James was struggling to contain his holiday excitement and became very distracted and disruptive in class. I had an all-too-necessary, private conversation with him. "James," I began, "I always reward effort in my classroom, but first I have to see it. Work with me here and this week will become much better for us both." Although James was not necessarily the model student for the remainder of the week, his obvious efforts were welcomed. That Friday afternoon he was on his way to the bus when I asked him to stay a moment after class. "I really appreciate all your effort this week, James. Are you trick-or-treating tomorrow?" I asked. "Yep," James began. "I'm gonna be a vampire." I handed him an instant camera and gave him some fun assignments as a reward for his weeklong efforts. "There are three pictures left, James. Take one and label it 'Ugly.' The second, label that one 'Scary.' And the third," and I reflected upon my youth and all that free candy I eagerly poured onto the carpet by night's end, "Label that third one 'Free.'"

With Monday morning came the return of my camera and the three requested pictures labeled accordingly. The photograph labeled "Ugly" was a picture of James, no costume, no smile, and apparently a self-portrait, a bit blurred since he was merely an arm's length away. The second, labeled "Scary," was a photograph of his new stepfather. The third, labeled "Free," had no candy in it at all—it was a picture of a pigeon perched on a fence post.

Until that moment, I had been under the assumption that James had everything in the world going for him, but I was wrong. You see, it is not in an eight-year-old's nature to simply approach his teacher and say, "Mr. G., you probably noticed my mom recently got remarried. I don't think this man likes me. He's mean to me and makes fun of me. He doesn't like for me to be around. But when I see how happy my mom is when she's around him, I know that means that she doesn't like for me to be around anymore, either."

That is very serious information coming from an eight-year-old child. And yet those words are exactly what James said to me with three photographs. The influence of visual communication goes far beyond the borders of a mere snapshot. Some things cannot be learned in a college program or a methods course—they must be taught to us by our students. Think of what *you* will learn from *your* students.

Friends' Gate

I had heard so many negative things concerning a new student, Jonathan, prior to his enrollment in my class that I chose not to review his records when they arrived. I felt that because he did not have to sift through my old baggage, perhaps I should not sift through his. I decided we would begin on unbiased, neutral grounds. I did choose, however, to read his medical and family background.

Jonathan was born in 1980 in Houston. After his mother abandoned him, his maternal grandmother and great-aunt raised him. Just before his eighth birthday, both women passed away and he returned to his mother. Without time to grieve his losses, Jonathan was introduced to his mother for the first time. In her absence, she had married a man with four children and given birth to four of her own. She basically announced, "I am your mother, this is your stepfather, and these are your eight brothers and sisters. We have arranged for you to be bused to another school beginning tomorrow. You will share a bedroom with your four stepbrothers."

During that school year, Jonathan had four teachers, no friends, and was labeled emotionally disturbed. This label qualified him for the program I was teaching at the time. Jonathan was unkempt in appearance, which did not seem to bother him, nor did it bother me. What did bother me was that he was extremely withdrawn, completely isolated. He had put himself into a bubble that no one was going to pop . . . except me.

One day I asked my students to select something to photograph with an instant camera. Once he had the camera in his hands, Jonathan burst through the classroom door and bee-lined to the bicycle rack. He took a photograph of the bicycle rack from the outside looking through the fence. Without saying a word, I reached in front of Jonathan, removed his photograph from the camera, and walked back to the classroom. I explained he must first draw and color his photograph before I allowed him to see it.

He drew a wonderful picture with colorful, imaginative simplicity, a yellow fence with a red bicycle behind it. I then asked him to title his new masterpiece. Without hesitation, Jonathan wrote "Friends' Gate" across the bottom of his drawing. The peculiarity of his title struck me. "Your photograph turned out perfect, Jonathan!" I began. "And your picture is every bit as nice, but I'm really excited about your title. Would you tell me something about it?" His response was a mere shrug of the shoulders. "You came up with a fabulous title without even taking the time to think it over. What does 'Friends' Gate' mean to you? I mean, why not 'Bike Rack' or 'Jonathan's Picture'? Why 'Friends' Gate'?" The second shrug of his shoulders told me that the interpretation of his title was personal to Jonathan. He realized I was suddenly penetrating his bubble and quickly pulled away.

Monday morning of the next week, I made my routine safety rounds of the school (I was the supervisor of the Safety Patrol program). On that particular morning, I was greeted by two overexcited student patrols who were upset with Jonathan. It seemed he was not complying with the school rule of retreating to the playground after getting off the bus. He was standing at the front corner of the building staring at the bike rack each day. I assured the patrols that I would personally attend to it. I felt the best approach would be for me to find somewhere that I could stare at the bicycle rack for a few days so I could assess Jonathan's fascination.

At the bicycle rack each day I witnessed the same group of children proudly wheeling their bicycles through the gate, their door to friendship. Once inside the gate, the students would assume a casual slouch against the fence or sit sidesaddle on their bicycle seats and engage in action-packed conversations with one another. The only students allowed inside the bicycle rack were those who rode bicycles to school. This, of course, added to the mystique of the clique.

It seemed clear to me what my next move should be. That evening, I searched for a used bicycle from a neighborhood teacher supply store (garage sale). The following morning, I remarked to Jonathan about the carelessness of a student who had left his bicycle at the side of the building and asked him to make sure the bicycle found its way to the bicycle rack. This particular bicycle, however, had the annoying, recurring habit of showing up each morning, so I had to enlist Jonathan's assistance each day. After three days, he casually exchanged conversation with the bicycle clique. Although Jonathan eventually uncovered my scheme, it seemed practical for him to become the newly appointed, supervising safety patrol of the school bicycle rack. I am pleased to report that Jonathan brought his new attitude into the classroom and began participating and socializing. He even started to do normal, silly things, like poking kids in line and throwing the occasional crust of bread across the cafeteria.

To Jonathan, inside "Friends' Gate" was a feeling of belonging. For the first time since the passing of his beloved grandmother and great-aunt, Jonathan felt like he could be a part of something once again. Two months later, Jonathan's family relocated and I never saw him again, but I will never forget my experiences with him. I took the opportunity to learn from him, and I am grateful for that. I can only hope to be as good a teacher as Jonathan was.

2 Brain-Compatible Learning

Brain-compatible learning is a dynamic, interdisciplinary, systemwide method of instruction based on the way current research in neuroscience suggests our brains naturally learn best. With technological advances such as positron emission tomography (PET) and magnetic resonance imaging (MRI), people now know far more about the functions of the brain than ever before. No longer forced to rely on 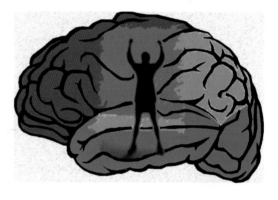 the brain of a cadaver, neuroscientists have embraced research that arms today's educators with the ability to design new strategies for the classroom. Educators are changing how they view their students and are adjusting their teaching styles accordingly. We used to believe that we only use 10 percent of our brains, and that one hemisphere of the brain dominates, so that we are either "left-brained" or "right-brained." During this past decade, scientists have disproved these beliefs and brought brain research to the forefront of education.

Understanding that the brain has a natural propensity to learn in certain ways has led to customized teaching strategies that have begun to overshadow the traditional cookie-cutter methods. Learning communities are becoming far more productive. Many states, such as Florida, Michigan, and South Dakota, have implemented districtwide initiatives that train teachers in the field of brain-compatible learning. They are trained to maximize instruction, enhance memory, increase learning of content, and implement cross-curricular teaching strategies. Studies show students learn better and retain more when their lessons are integrated with music and drama, direct experiences, emotion, and real-world context

(Campbell, 1997). The more regions of the brain that are involved and the more students employ their emotions during learning, the more channels they have for recalling information.

Research demonstrates that the brain functions best with the following concepts: teamwork, a positive classroom environment, sufficient processing time, preference, meaningful subject matter, the absence of threat, instant feedback, and mastery (Marzano, Pickering, & Pollack, 2001).

- **Teamwork** promotes a sense of community in the classroom. Students assume ownership of a communal process as individuals who share equal parts of the whole.
- A **positive classroom environment** might include live plants, the essence of fragrant oils, a comfortable room temperature, natural light or full-spectrum lighting, complementary colors that influence learning, and nonlyrical music selected specifically for its tempo.
- **Sufficient processing time** allows students to discover and explore patterns and make connections in the learning process. Students need time to create sequential steps toward mastering objectives. This also enables them to process concepts and apply these new processing skills to their world.
- **Preference** gives students opportunities to select how they may best learn the material. This is particularly important when nurturing individually identified multiple intelligences while continuing to build bridges to any underdeveloped intelligences.
- **Meaningful subject matter** should match the students' age level and be the doorway to lifelong learning skills. The content not only must be relevant to their future, but also must appeal to their interests.
- The **absence of threat** alleviates fears or anxieties caused by classroom expectations, rigorous schedules, poor life skills, and stressful peer interactions.
- **Instant feedback** lets students check their own levels of comprehension. It provides them opportunities to make continuous adjustments throughout the lesson.
- **Mastery** gives students knowledge about their own thoughts as well as the factors that influence their thinking. Student-based portfolios and authentic assessments are excellent methods to demonstrate student mastery and retention.

There is a restlessness afoot among some parents and educators who feel that visual learners are neglected in the school system. So, you may ask, does brain research support such a thing as a "Visual Learner"? Yes. But it's not a single type. Visual learning is more like a kaleidoscope than a single shade of a color.

That's because there is a remarkable diversity to the organization of visual abilities in the brain. Expertise at visual learning may mean a preference for learning by seeing visual relationships or pictures, a preference for learning by reading text, expertise at translating verbal information into visual pictures or imagining visual permutations, visual sensitivity to detail, color, texture, or motion, or a spectacular memory for visual information.

—Bruce Landon, Douglas College Psychology Department (Landon, 2005)

The following tools can help you deliver content to your students in a brain-compatible way:

- visuals
- visual thinking maps (see Chapter 5)
- visual links (see Chapter 5)
- visual journals (see Chapter 5)
- drawing and artwork (see Chapter 4)
- graphic organizers (see Chapter 3)
- movement and dance (see Chapter 4)
- music and rhythm (see Chapter 4)
- creative writing (metaphors, similes, analogies) (see Chapter 6)
- writing journals (see Chapter 5)
- mnemonic strategies
- mentoring and cooperative learning
- photography, imagery, and symbols (see Chapter 3)
- role playing (see Chapter 4)
- peer-to-peer teaching
- manipulatives
- critical visual thinking (see Chapter 1)
- problem solving
- field trips
- guest speakers
- games
- brainstorming

LEARNING STYLES

Three specific categories of learning styles naturally blend with brain-compatible learning: cognitive, affective, and physiological.

The cognitive learning style reflects the "thinking" components: left-brain/right-brain, reflective/impulsive, and analytical/relational. Cognitive learning also includes a sociological component: concept of self, partner, and group. Cognitive learning theories support the use of imagery combined with the written word as an influential means for teaching literacy skills. In a study comparing multimodal lessons using text and pictures with unimodal text-only written instructions, the students had significantly improved performance with the former than with the latter (Gellevij, Van-der-Meij, deJong, & Pieters, 2002). As Aristotle once stated, "Without image, thinking is impossible." There are several activities you can try in a classroom environment to foster cognitive diversity.

- Assign tasks that students can complete within their ability to pay sustained attention.
- Incorporate active assignments using bodily-kinesthetic and analytical behaviors.
- Encourage students to reflect prior to responding to a question, be it oral or written.
- Provide assignments that elicit analysis and organization.

The affective learning style is about emotion: self-confidence, motivation, and diligence. What can you do to cultivate affective diversity?

- Promote a personal approach with students.
- Associate concepts to personal experiences and interests.
- Model what you teach.
- Use materials to elicit expression of feelings.
- Accentuate holistic explanations prior to focusing on particular details.
- Personalize the curriculum.
- Use humor, drama, and role-play.
- Incorporate cooperative learning.

The physiological learning style brings brain-compatible learning full circle. Here the emphasis is on the learning environment: lighting, sound, temperature, physical structure, and classroom arrangement. However, it goes beyond where the students learn—it focuses on the physical needs of the students themselves. How do they perceive their environment? What time of day is it? Are they hungry? What is their body language? Are they ready for some movement? Here are some suggestions to foster physiological diversity in the classroom setting.

- Rotate seating arrangement, monitor the temperature of the classroom, and be in tune with the lighting. Melatonin is a sleep-related hormone secreted by the pineal gland in the brain. It suppresses endorphins, which are the neurotransmitters found in the brain that relieve pain and produce feelings of euphoria. Natural light suppresses melatonin and positively affects the learning brain.

- Do not wait until the end of the lesson to check for comprehension. Check frequently in planned intervals.

- Allow a wait time for students' responses, whether oral or written.

- Be aware of the learning modalities. Challenge yourself to tap into the visual, auditory, and tactile-kinesthetic modalities on a continuous basis.

DIFFERENTIATING INSTRUCTION

What may be an enriching learning environment for one student may not be for another. It is important to teach students to think for themselves; no two children are alike, nor do any two children have identical learning styles. Learning must be differentiated to be effective.

Differentiating instruction occurs when teachers produce several avenues to challenge the needs of students of varying aptitudes and learning requirements. This instructional approach gives the students a sense of ownership over the learning process and focuses strictly on individual needs. It is also an effective gateway to integrating more technology into the classroom.

Before differentiating instruction, teachers should conduct an informal needs assessment using various performance indicators. Some students will be on level, just as some will be above and some below. For this reason, you can differentiate instruction by providing four learning options. The mandated curricula elements will be consistent with all students, while the actual intricacies of the content, activities, and objectives will vary. This ensures each student will be challenged while decreasing the likelihood of frustration.

Here are four methods to differentiate instruction.

1. Differentiating the elements and theme. The elements of instruction become the knowledge and skills we want our students to obtain. The rate at which the students acquire the knowledge should be based on the individual results of the needs assessment.

2. Differentiating the methods and activities. By offering alternative learning paths, you provide individual ownership. We know that 65 percent of your students are visual learners. Therefore, use graphic organizers, visual thinking maps, flowcharts, visual mapping, visual links, and visual journals to exhibit their comprehension. Not only does this become a visual record of their success, it is also authentic assessment and can be used in students' portfolios.

3. Differentiating the outcome. Changing the elements of the outcome gives students choices. Higher-functioning students should be motivated to pursue many choices, while lower-functioning students may choose a few. What is important to remember is that the main outcome will meet the standards of the curricula.

4. Differentiating by changing the learning environment.

   Movement and downtime

   Natural light

   Background music

   A classroom temperature of sixty-eight to seventy-two degrees

   Integration of the effects of color

   Integration of the effects of aromas

   Peer-to-peer interaction

   Focus on multiple intelligences and learning styles

Some suggestions for differentiating instruction in the classroom follow:

Modify questions.

Provide alternative activities.

Use cooperative learning.

Alter the pace of instruction.

Use multitiered assignments.

Be aware of individual students' interests.

Encourage individual projects.

Use learning contracts.

Provide learning centers.

Provide for the students' learning needs to ensure they feel the instruction is worthy of their time and energy.

MULTIPLE INTELLIGENCES

Howard Gardner is a Hobbs Professor of Cognition and Education at the Harvard Graduate School of Education and adjunct professor of neurology at the Boston University School of Medicine. In 1983, Gardner published *Frames of Mind: The Theory of Multiple Intelligences*, a work stemming from his early interests in psychology and the social sciences. Since then, Gardner has identified eight different intelligences. He believes the brain has all eight intelligences, as described below. Some of these may not be developed, however, or may be underdeveloped due to lack of life experiences.

Verbal-linguistic intelligence involves spoken and written language, along with the ability to learn languages and use them to accomplish goals. Although this encompasses reading, speaking, listening, and writing, being linguistically intelligent does not require highly developed skills in each of the four areas. These students are your readers, your talkers, your poets, and storytellers. Possible future professions: poet, teacher, translator, writer, politician, lawyer, journalist.

Activities to foster the verbal-linguistic intelligence

- Making presentations
- Making speeches
- Role-playing
- Listening to tapes while reading

Logical-mathematical intelligence involves investigating issues scientifically, analyzing problems logically, and carrying out mathematical operations. Strong in science and math, the logical-mathematical intelligence seeks patterns, thinks logically, and reasons deductively. These students are your scientists and mathematicians, and are attracted to technology. Possible future professions: scientist, researcher, computer programmer, engineer, accountant, mathematician.

Activities to foster logical-mathematical intelligence

- Working on the computer
- Writing applications
- Sorting objects
- Taking apart or fixing gadgets
- Solving puzzles and mysteries

Musical-rhythmic intelligence involves appreciation of musical patterns and skill in composition and performance. Closely related to verbal-linguistic intelligence, musical-rhythmic intelligence encompasses the ability to recognize and compose musical pitches, tones, and rhythms. These students hum and tap their way through thinking. Possible future professions: musician, singer, composer, disc jockey.

Activities to foster the musical-rhythmic intelligence

- Listening to background or environmental music
- Playing musical instruments
- Listening to musical performances

Bodily-kinesthetic intelligence involves the ability to use mental capacities to direct bodily movement. This intelligence taps into the skill of using one's whole body or various parts of the body to solve problems. These students like to use their hands. They are the doers who enjoy and perhaps require lots of physical activity. Possible future professions: athlete, dancer, physical education teacher, actor, artisan, firefighter.

Activities to foster the bodily-kinesthetic intelligence

- Stretching
- Role-playing
- Building models
- Exercising and dancing

Visual-spatial intelligence involves the ability to recognize and use the patterns of both wide space and confined areas. These students are your visual thinkers and artists. Possible future professions: architect, inventor, navigator, engineer, interior designer, visual artist, sculptor.

Activities to foster the visual-spatial intelligence

- Working with art materials
- Changing locations
- Watching videos, films, and theater

Interpersonal intelligence is the ability to understand what motivates others in their intentions and desires. It supports the ability to work successfully and collaboratively with others. These students are your group leaders and gravitate to instruction through cooperative learning. Possible future professions: counselor, businessperson, salesperson, politician.

Activities to foster the interpersonal intelligence

- Competing
- Playing interactive games
- Working on teams

- Learning cooperatively
- Collaborating and practicing empathy

Intrapersonal intelligence involves the ability to understand oneself, and one's fears, feelings, and motivations. These students prefer to tackle the job independently. Possible future professions: researcher, counselor, theorist.

Activities to foster the intrapersonal intelligence

- Practicing thinking strategies
- Visualizing imagery
- Writing in a journal

Naturalist intelligence involves the ability to distinguish and compare both manufactured and natural things. It entails identifying and categorizing various components of the environment. These students long for the outdoors, outside activities, and field trips. Possible future professions: scientist, speech therapist, composer, architect.

Activities to foster the naturalist intelligence

- Using numerical, geometrical, and musical patterns
- Using linguistic and behavioral patterns

At this time, Gardner is also exploring the inclusion of additional future intelligences: spiritual intelligence, existential intelligence, and moral intelligence.

Mindy L. Kornhaber, who conducted research with Howard Gardner, stated that "the theory validates educators' everyday experience: students think and learn in many different ways. It also provides educators with a conceptual framework for organizing and reflecting on curriculum assessment and pedagogical practices. In turn, this reflection has led many educators to develop new approaches that might better meet the needs of the range of learners in their classrooms" (Kornhaber, 2001, 276). The key to recognizing multiple intelligences is finding the areas in which your students are intelligent, and then nurturing them through customized teaching strategies. Find ways to tap into those areas where students are underdeveloped and begin building bridges through activities in the classroom.

CHARACTER EDUCATION

My son Sean is twenty-five years old. Compared with my generation growing up, he and his generation spent three to five times as much time in front of a television, had less than half the amount of unstructured playtime, spent one-third of the amount of time outdoors, spent 100 percent more time on computers and video game toys, and had three times as much adult-managed playtime. In contrast, when I was a young boy, I'd spring from the bed on any given summer's Saturday morning, dump half a box of cereal into a large Tupperware salad bowl, add half a quart of milk, and plant myself on the braided oval rug in our living room. Once the screen warmed-up on our black-and-white television, I had the arduous task of choosing which of two stations to watch. Back then, cartoons were once a week and generally ran no later than 10:30 a.m., at which point I would rinse the bowl, grab my baseball glove and ball, saddle-up the Stingray, and peddle down to the vacant lot in our neighborhood. There several friends would greet me and we would choose teams and prepare for a daylong marathon of baseball. Since I particularly liked playing second base, I was quick to proclaim, "I'm playing second base!" at which point a friend would veto, "No, you'll be playing left field." "Do you understand whose ball this is?," I'd retort. "And do you understand whose bat this is?," he'd reply. Suddenly we were confronted with a dilemma that meant there was to be no baseball for the day. Since there were no adults in our presence to solve the problem, we had to muster our infinite wisdom and compromise. In other words, we had to solve our own problem. Coupled with the fact that today's youth has three times as much adult-managed playtime, this scenario makes it easy to understand why today's youth has such difficulty with conflict resolution.

Students spend more waking hours during the school year with their teachers than with their parents. Character education needs to be a warp thread woven into each school day, each school moment. It should not simply be injected on a need-to-need basis. In order for teachers to prepare their students for the world in which they live, character education is critical.

It is difficult to define character education in a few words. There are, however, standards that appear in most descriptions. These standards help prepare character education programs that are vital to the vast umbrella we call our education system.

Ethics. Expressing caring, honesty, fairness, responsibility, and respect for self and others.

Holistic. Developing the cognitive, behavioral, and emotional aspects of moral development.

Comprehensive. Using all facets of schooling, such as students' relationships with peers, teachers, and school staff, while addressing student diversity.

Community. Fostering a school community that promotes the desire to learn and the desire to be a good person.

Moral Development. Assessing "real-life" situations to guide in good moral decision making.

Curriculum. Ensuring that the school curricula contain the warp thread of character education.

Motivation. Creating an environment for students to earn self-esteem, as opposed to being given a self. There is a difference between being told you are a good person and doing the right thing when no one is looking.

Modeling. Demonstrating strong character so students can model it. The simple act of a teacher holding a door for a student can go a long way.

Leadership. Taking part in class meetings, student government, peer mediation, cross-age tutoring, and student-led initiatives.

Family. Reaching out to parents and extended family to assist and reinforce the character education initiative.

Evaluation. Designing an action plan to continually assess the character of the school, faculty's growth as character educators, and the character of the student body.

In the end, actions speak louder than words. Students are inundated with reality TV, and are often plagued with the modeled problems and negative behaviors that unfortunately lurk in the shadows of character education. When students are presented with opportunities to visualize the upside of character education, however, they will begin building values and moral development, which encourages them to be courageous, show respect, be fair, take responsibility, hold on to their integrity, and be honest.

THE SIX STAGES OF MORAL DEVELOPMENT

Lawrence Kohlberg (1927–1987) was a psychologist and professor at the University of Chicago and Harvard University. He was the thirtieth most eminent psychologist of the twentieth century (Haggbloom, et al., 2002). Following in the footsteps of Swiss philosopher, natural scientist, and developmental psychologist Jean Piaget (1896–1980), Kohlberg's research led to the formulation of the six stages of moral development, with each stage more sufficient than the last at responding to moral dilemmas. Moral development is truly the backbone of character education. By leading students through discussions involving moral dilemmas, teachers can walk them through each stage without their knowledge. Teachers can then pinpoint each stage in revisiting the discussion. This enables students to construct moral development on their own, as opposed to being "told" what is right and what is wrong.

Before the stages are introduced, teachers should read a short story to the class. Kohlberg's study used the following story:

"Heinz Steals the Drug"

In Europe, a woman was near death from a special kind of cancer. There was one drug that the doctors thought might save her. It was a form of radium that a drug-gist in the same town had recently discovered. The drug was expensive to make, but the druggist was charging ten times what the drug cost him to make. He paid $200 for the radium and charged $2,000 for a small dose of the drug. The sick woman's husband, Heinz, went to everyone he knew to borrow the money, but he could only get together about $1,000, which is half of what it cost. He told the druggist that his wife was dying and asked him to sell it cheaper or let him pay later. But the druggist said: "No, I discovered the drug and I'm going to make money from it." So Heinz got desperate and broke into the man's store to steal the drug for his wife. (Kohlberg, 1963, p. 19)

Now ask the students, "Should the husband have done that?" Each student comes from a different background and each response is his or her own opinion, so there are no incorrect answers. Ultimately, their answers will form a processing chain that will lead them through all six stages of Kohlberg's moral development. Ask guiding questions that highlight each stage. Once each stage is covered, introduce the stages to the students and review examples from the discussion so they understand what stage they were in and why.

Stage 1. Obedience and Punishment Orientation

Kohlberg's students responded to the question with statements like, "It's against the law," or "It's bad to steal." When asked to expand their thoughts, they dwelled on the consequences, stating that theft is wrong and "You'll get punished."

Activity

Ask students to close their eyes and describe the first visual that comes to mind when they hear the word "steal" or "theft."

Stage 2. Individualism and Exchange

One of Kohlberg's students said Heinz stole the drug because he and his wife had children and he needed her to be well enough to care for them. If the drug did not help her, though, this student pointed out, the theft would leave the children without parents: one terminally ill and the other in prison.

Activity

Ask students to describe a visual using self-generated mental imagery of Heinz in prison, the wife in the hospital bed, and the children alone.

Stage 3. Good Interpersonal Relationships

"He was a good man for wanting to save her," and "His intentions were good, that of saving the life of someone he loves." Kohlberg's students also felt that even if Heinz did not love his wife, he should still steal the drug. "I don't think any husband should sit back and watch his wife die."

Activity

Ask students to recall something they had seen in a movie, television, or an actual incident that would exemplify the context of this stage.

Stage 4. Maintaining the Social Order

"It's wrong to steal," or "It's against the law." Again, Kohlberg's students echoed their thinking from Stage 1, and again they could not elaborate, with the exception of repeating that stealing can get you put in jail. The students understand the concept of the functions of the law for society as a whole.

Activity

Ask students to assign a color to their thoughts. For example, stealing is red, or freedom is green, etc.

Stage 5. Social Contract and Individual Rights

It is the husband's responsibility to save his wife. Her life is at risk, which surpasses any other measurement one might use to judge his actions. A human life is more important than property and money. It is interesting that, generally, legal and moral positions concur but here they conflict.

Kohlberg's students felt the judge should regard the moral position more heavily by imposing a lighter sentence while preserving the legal law.

Activity

Create a concept development organizer, which is a flowchart version of a graphic organizer, of the five stages before moving on to the sixth.

Stage 6. Universal Principles

Martin Luther King Jr. believed laws are only viable insofar as they are grounded in justice. A loyalty to justice carries with it a moral imperative to disobey unjust laws. Naturally, King understood the general need for laws and the democratic processes (as seen in Stages 4 and 5), and he was willing to accept the penalties for his actions. In spite of that, he felt that the higher principle of justice required civil disobedience.

Activity

Watch the movie *John Q*, staring Denzel Washington, who plays a down-on-his-luck father whose insurance will not cover his son's heart transplant. Washington's character takes the hospital's emergency room hostage until the doctors agree to perform the operation.

Teachers should periodically revisit moral development using actual events from their own lives or current events.

Activity

Choose three students from the class (i.e., Mike, JoAnne, and Chris). JoAnne works at a fast-food restaurant. One day Chris comes in to eat lunch. Chris does not have enough money, so asks JoAnne for a "free" cheeseburger and soda. Since Chris is a good friend and has done plenty of favors for JoAnne in the past, JoAnne would like to help. Since the manager, Mike, is not around, she thinks no one will know. However, she knows that it is technically stealing. JoAnne is not sure what to do.

- Chris believes this situation is merely asking a friend for some help. What do you think of this way of looking at things? Why?
- Since Chris has done many favors for JoAnne in the past, would it be fair for JoAnne not to return a favor in this situation?
- Again, this is stealing. The restaurant is a large chain, though, and sells thousands of cheeseburgers daily. Obviously, little harm is being caused to the restaurant in order to provide a good friend with lunch. Isn't that fair?

The key to resolving this situation is to have students visualize themselves in the shoes of the characters in the story. There are some great books that will naturally stimulate similar discussions on moral development: *Charlie and the Chocolate Factory* (Roald Dahl), *Bunnicula: A Rabbit Tale of Mystery* (Deborah Howe et al.) and *Bridge to Terabithia* (Katherine Paterson).

PROCESSING VISUAL INFORMATION

It is estimated that the brain contains 100 billion neurons that create more than 1,000 trillion synaptic contact points (junctions between two nerve cells, where the tip of a nerve fiber almost touches another cell in order to transmit signals). This number is estimated to be greater than all the stars and planets in all the galaxies (Diamond, 1999; Healy, 1994). During the first month of an infant's life, the number of synapses increases from 50 trillion to 1 quadrillion. To provide a visual, if that same infant's body grew at a comparable rate, his or her weight would increase from 8.5 pounds to 170 pounds by the age of one month.

The visual cortex constitutes about 20 percent of the entire cerebral cortex. It is located in the occipital lobe, or lower region of the brain's hemispheres. It is highly specialized for processing information about static and moving objects, and is excellent in pattern recognition. It is made up of six layers and can be subdivided into more than thirty specialized areas. Each area communicates with its neighbors by using more than two hundred linkages. This area of the brain processes information from the retina. It is a direct map of the field of vision, organized spatially in the same fashion as the retina itself. Forty percent of all nerve fibers connected to the brain are linked to the retina. In fact, more than 90 percent of all the information that comes to the brain is visual. In just one hour, more than thirty-six thousand visuals may be registered in the brain (Hyerle, 2000). At least 30 million neurons in the entire visual cortex are activated by the single image of a house or a face (Levy, Hasson, and Malach, 2004).

People are able to recognize and extract the gist of a scene—its core meaning—in less than one-tenth of a second. Research conducted by the 3M Corporation found the brain processes visuals sixty thousand times faster than it processes text; visual aids in a classroom have been found to improve learning by up to 400 percent (3M Corporation, 2001). Cells in the visual cortex distinguish between light and dark and eventually condense the information into an image that the brain can distinguish. As humans, we tend to dismiss the awesome power of the visual cortex. With a mere blink of an eye, we have information playing like a movie before our very eyes. With a mere click of a shutter, a camera freezes the information and stores it as raw data. In contrast, the visual cortex must first interpret the information, sending it to at least thirty specialized areas dispersed throughout the brain that are dedicated to one kind of feature discrimination or another—size, shape, color, or orientation (Ratey, 2001). When you are witness to a large green truck speeding past, your brain is separately processing its color, shape, location, and direction of motion. Is it stored in short-term memory? Long-term memory? Instantly discarded as insignificant? Did it stimulate a physiological response such as perspiration or a tear? Did it elicit an emotion of fear, joy, or sadness? In an experimental study, students were tested on their recall of instructional text. The study compared text accompanied by visual imagery and abstract verbal text. The findings concluded that using the concreteness of visual imagery was the variable overwhelmingly linked to successful comprehension and recall (Sadoski & Paivio, 2002).

Visual perception is an interpretive act involving analysis and awareness. It plays an important role in allowing humans to respond to their surrounding environments. We analyze our environment based on patterns, forms, and objects. The information is in the form of color, texture, depth, motion, and point of reference. This information takes on a conscious meaning referred to as visual awareness. Visual information is encoded and processed by the brain's language centers (Restak, 2003). Visual perception must also decipher information with unconscious meanings such as illusions where we lose our point of reference or subliminal advertising for commercial products.

As a definition, visual processing represents a set of skills used to interpret and understand visual information. When a student is required to copy something written on a chalkboard, that student must use visual memory to recall what was seen, then use visual motor integration to accurately copy the information. Many students with learning disabilities have trouble learning because of a breakdown in the areas of visual spatial, visual analysis, or visual motor skills.

A basketball coach demonstrated a drill for a high school student who was trying out for the team. It was important that the drill be performed correctly or it would interfere with the performance of the other participating players. After several unsuccessful attempts, the player asked to see the playbook. Upon review of the diagrams, the student performed the task with little effort. In this case, the player needed to rely on visual analysis because visual motor skills alone were not able to secure success. The following will give you an idea of what took place in the student's visual cortex:

visual acuity: optimal vision of 20/20 with or without correction

eye alignment: aligning both eyes to accurately track the ever-changing position and location of the ball

depth perception: aligning both eyes to accurately identify the position in space of the ball and the other players

eye flexibility: binocular eye movements constantly shifting quickly and accurately from near to far

visual recognition: visually processing the angles, speed, and rotation of the ball, position of the players on the court, and the position of the boundary lines and goals

visual memory: based on previous visual information, gives the student a sense of court awareness and allows the student to initiate offensive and defensive movements

visual tracking: eye movements enabling the student to scan the entire playing area and monitor the location of the ball

eye–hand–body coordination: coordinating motor movements based on the input of visual information—the eyes leading the body

A great way to assist your students on improving their visual processing skills is to teach them juggling. Mastering the skill increases the amount of grey matter in areas of the brain that process and store visual information. Although once thought impossible, we now know that new stimuli can alter the brain's structure. "Researchers at the University of Rochester found that young adults who regularly played video games full of high-speed car chases and blazing gun battles showed better visual skills than those who did not. They also found that people who do not normally play video games but were trained to play them developed enhanced visual perception" (CNN, 2003). Any eye–hand art-related task unfamiliar to your students can produce similar results. These tasks can be a direct pathway to the visual information processing system.

VISUAL VS. AUDITORY CORTEX

When I conduct training seminars, I do an activity to demonstrate the power the visual learning modality has over the auditory modality. I begin by asking a participant to describe a simple drawing consisting of basic and adjoining geometric shapes. The participants are to create the drawing based on its description. Although it appears to be a relatively simple task, I do impose a few rules on the person giving the description. I ask the participant to turn away from the audience and to use no gesticulations. At the conclusion of the activity, I display the diagram on a screen for the participants. Laughter, moans, and groans are the typical responses. Many give up, or simply fail to create a facsimile of the diagram. All forms of visual learning are removed and the participants may only rely on the auditory information. In contrast, part two of this activity is to put the participants in pairs. They are instructed to take one minute each to share information on themselves (Married? Children? Favorite foods? Pets? Hobbies? Number of years in teaching? Subject or grade level being taught?). Again, there are some imposed rules. They may not speak, write, or use props. After two minutes, the participants speak to the group and tell them about their new friend. The information that is communicated in one minute, relying solely on visual modality, is amazing. It is an excellent illustration of how much more powerful the visual component to learning is over auditory learning. This is also a wonderful activity for your classroom.

Auditory information is transitory—it is there and then it is gone. Auditory information may disappear before students have a chance to pay attention long enough to take in what is being said. Students may be accurately interpreting only fragments of auditory messages.

Visual information stays there long enough for the student to see it, take in the information, and respond to it. Students can go back over and over if they need to so they can understand and remember. Do your students prefer oral or written instructions? Would they prefer an art history lesson or an artist as a guest speaker? Are they better at remembering names or faces? Would it be easier for them to learn new information using words or pictures? Lectures or film and video? Radio news or newspapers and the Internet? How-to demonstrations or printed manuals? The answers to these questions help you understand whom you are teaching. Perhaps, and more than likely, you will find a mixed audience of learners. That is a good thing, provided you are prepared to embrace each student's dominant learning modality and correlate your teaching strategies to meet all students' needs.

A seventh-grade teacher reflected on a student from her second-period science class. His name was David. He was blind from birth and sought the attention of his peers by being surly and disruptive. His teacher's philosophy had always emphasized that if a door ever closes on one of her students it became her job to find an open window. These "windows of opportunity," as she referred to them, were always there if she looked hard enough.

The absence of one of a person's five senses leaves the remaining four to fill the void. In many cases, the other senses' functional values increase due to the brain's desire to compensate for the severity of the loss. It became increasingly apparent that David had incredible auditory perception that had developed due to his lack of sight.

Early in the semester, David's teacher learned just how fine-tuned his hearing had become. He was sitting alone as he listened to his neighboring cooperative learning group discussing an activity. They were engaged in a science project that involved the use of an instant camera. The students were assigning the job roles needed to meet the objective of the lesson. Much to the surprise of his classmates, David suddenly volunteered to be the photographer. The classroom went silent and a student from his group reluctantly handed him the camera. All eyes went to the teacher for intervention. She smiled and nodded with approval.

The groups were instructed to make an image of a potted plant that had matured and blossomed. David asked his group's Facilitator to tap a pencil on the clay pot. David pressed the camera against his forehead just above the bridge of his nose. As the Facilitator tapped the pot, David moved his head to the left, and then slightly to the right, then asked his classmate to step out of the picture prior to squeezing the trigger. When the image ejected from the front of the camera, he reached out and held the picture of the potted plant in his hand. The group's Recorder asked if she could see the photograph as it developed, then genuinely praised David for the quality of the image. It was exactly what they needed for the lesson. It was unanimous: David was to be the group's Visual Recorder—their photographer. In that moment, David's teacher watched as he was acknowledged, rewarded, and praised by his peers for a skill that seemed to elude him. David's enriched auditory ability allowed him to communicate visually through his auditory perception skills. Most important was the response shared by six of his peers. David had a new way to communicate, one that was not given to him at birth. He used his strengths to overcome a weakness. Although he was unable to decode an image, he had now found his ability to encode, to use photography as a language, and to increase his learning skills through visual communication. Needless to say, his teacher and his classmates had helped David find a key to a door that had always been closed.

As an exclamation point to the story, a few years later David's teacher was married. David arrived at the reception with camera in hand. His teacher will tell you, "It is my most valued photo album, commemorating not just my wonderful wedding day, but also my decision to become a teacher. David is truly a 'gifted' child. It just took him a little longer to unwrap his presents. He may not have sight, but he definitely has vision."

RIGHT-BRAIN AND LEFT-BRAIN

The section of the brain that controls rational functions—the cerebral cortex—is made of two halves. These are linked by masses of nerve fibers that allow information to pass between them. These halves are generally called the right-brain and the left-brain, but the technical term is hemispheres. Scientific studies show that signals coming into the brain are automatically sorted in a level of the brain stem. The information is then sent to the hemisphere that the sorting mechanisms believe is "in charge," the level that can best handle that type of information (Levy, Trevarthen, & Sperry, 1972). For some reason, our right and left hemispheres control the opposite sides of our bodies, so the right hemisphere controls our left side and processes what we see in our left eye, while the left hemisphere controls the right side and processes what we see in our right eye. Brain dominance refers to a preference for using one hemisphere of the brain over the other hemisphere. Traditionally, the left hemisphere of the brain was thought to be rational, analytical, and verbal, while the right hemisphere was thought to be holistic and intuitive, responsive to visual imagery. Although this information remains controversial, some researchers are leaning toward a lateral thinking brain that actually switches dominance (deBono, 1970). Our educational system seems to favor a left-brain style, with an exception being activities that involve creativity. Right-brain students prefer pictures, diagrams, charts, videos, discussing feelings, social activities, music, attention to the "overall picture," and creative projects. Left-brain learners prefer ample reading, writing, assignments involving reasoning and analyzing, attention to detail, quantitative methods, organized approaches to lessons, and a syllabus showing what will happen when. A study conducted in Germany noted that often people with right hemisphere brain damage who cannot mark the center of a horizontal line have no difficulty marking the center of a square. They used MRI to realize that line judgment activates only the right cortex (parietal region), while finding the center of a square activates the lingual gyrus in both brain hemispheres. The study concluded that the more object-like one makes a visual stimulus, the larger the brain regions accountable for interpretation. The implications of the study suggest the use of manipulatives and diagrams whenever possible for simple abstract concepts and for involvement of more of the brain (Fink et al., 2000).

Tapping in to both hemispheres is critical since relying on one hemisphere can cause negative aspects on learning. For example, teaching solely to the right-brain can cause an inability to articulate meanings or intentions, lack of responsiveness to learning goals or verbal ambiguity, and overly emotional responses. Alternatively, teaching solely to the left-brain might cause thinking within the box, or logical safe answers based on previous knowledge, and literal symbolization. As educators, we must ask ourselves certain questions: How do we tap into both hemispheres of the minds of our students? How do we teach to the whole brain as an integrated unit? The answer may very well lie in Leonardo da Vinci's Principles for the Development of a Complete Mind.

1. Study the science of art.

2. Study the art of science.

3. Develop your senses—especially learn how to see.

4. Realize that everything connects to everything else (Buzan & Buzan, 1996).

TAPPING IN TO THE RIGHT-BRAIN

Many people struggle with lateral thinking due to their cognitive comfort zone. They are most confident in their ability to process from a dominant hemisphere. Traditionally, the worlds of business, mathematics, engineering, and medical science are associated with left-brain thinking. If professionals in those fields were able to somehow shift their thought by drawing from the right-brain, their rational, verbal, and analytical modes would be complemented by their visual and perceptual modes. An exercise created by Dr. Betty Edwards enables most people to tap in to the right-brain and broaden their thinking by building the bridge between hemispheres to facilitate lateral thinking.

Dr. Edwards conducted research while teaching at California State University. She founded the Center for the Educational Applications of Brain Hemisphere Research. In her 1979 book, *Drawing on the Right Side of the Brain,* Edwards suggests exercises to bring out the creative abilities associated with the right side of the brain. Although she has devoted her teaching to drawing, painting, art history, and color theory, she also has consulted with major national and international corporations to heighten creative problem solving.

Dr. Edward's method of tapping in to the right side of the brain is a simple yet important technique in developing lateral thinking. While drawing a picture of a person from a photograph or other drawing, our left-brain labels the elements of the drawing, such as fingers, nose, and mouth. This creates conflict with the visual and perceptual thinking and we try to recreate the extremities or facial features as we know them. We are often unsatisfied with our work. However, when what we are drawing is presented to us upside-down, the visual clues no longer match. The brain becomes confused and unable to pinpoint and label the elements. What was a "nose" when presented in the upright orientation becomes a slanted line, angle to the right, then turning to the left. What was once a "mouth" becomes parallel lines curling upward on either side. The shift from left-brain to right-brain begins by eliminating the need to analyze and verbalize what is seen. We are no longer drawing a picture of a person: we are simply copying a series of lines and shadows.

When using the upside-down method with students, you will need a blank sheet of paper, a pencil, and a picture or drawing. Drawings copied from children's coloring books work well. Place the drawing upside-down on the desk in front of the student. Play soft music at a low level to create atmospheric wallpaper. It is important that there are no vocals or lyrics in the music because this would cause the students to remain in the left-brain to process the vocabulary. For this reason, it is also important that there be no talking during the course of the activity. The finished drawing will also be upside-down. Around twenty-two minutes into the activity, for most students the music will vanish, which is a sign that they have made the complete shift to the right-brain. Once the drawings are complete, have the students turn both sketches to the upright orientation. Most of your students will be pleasantly surprised at how well they did. Although this activity appears to be an art lesson on teaching drawing, it is actually designed to experience escaping mental paralysis or left-brain/right-brain conflict. Ask students how they felt during the exercise. This activity not only improves lateral thinking, but also enhances self-esteem. Ask a class of kindergartners how many are artists and all hands go up. Ask that same question of a group of fifth graders and you might see four or five hands go up.

DYSLEXIA

According to the International Dyslexia Association (IDA) and National Institute of Child Health and Human Development (NICHD), "Dyslexia is a specific learning disability that is neurological in origin. It is characterized by difficulties with accurate and/or fluent word recognition and by poor spelling and decoding abilities. These difficulties typically result from a deficit in the phonological component of language that is often unexpected in relation to other cognitive abilities and the provision of effective classroom instruction. Secondary consequences may include problems in reading comprehension and reduced reading experience that can impede growth of vocabulary and background knowledge" (IDA, 2002). Many professionals believe faulty "wiring" in the brain causes dyslexia, resulting in difficulties with phonological processing, or the mastery, storage, and retrieval of sounds and symbols. Dyslexia is determined  through a comprehensive diagnostic evaluation and can range from mild to severe. A commonly used evaluative instrument is the Nelson-Denny Reading Test, or the Gray Oral Readings Tests, fourth edition (GORT-4).

Dyslexia causes many weaknesses, such as

misnomia, or difficulty with word retrieval;

difficulty recalling names of people or places;

difficulty with oral reading;

an absence of fluency; and

extreme effort in reading and in spelling words.

People with dyslexia may have weaknesses, but they also have strengths, such as

the ability to think outside the box;

flexibility and adaptability;

ability to think broadly, to see the "big picture";

capability of learning, as observed in specialized areas and oral expression; and

extraordinary empathy.

Many famous people were diagnosed with or showed symptoms of dyslexia, most notably Cher, Agatha Christie, Winston Churchill, Tom Cruise, Leonardo da Vinci, Thomas Edison, Albert Einstein, Danny Glover, Magic Johnson, George Patton, W. B. Yeats, and Loretta Young (Davis Dyslexic Association International, n.d.), to name a few. All of these people had two things in common. First, few would have anticipated their eventual success. Second, in each instance there was someone, such as a parent, teacher, or coach, who openly believed in him or her, thereby helping the person develop an ardent interest in an area in which success could be found.

Although their distinctive brain architecture causes problems with reading, writing, and spelling, people with dyslexia shift to the right-brain to find their skills. They have vivid imaginations. They are curious and intuitive, with strong people skills, musical ability, athletic ability, and mechanical ability. However, in a classroom they feel as if they are driving in a foreign country.

Although it is important for teachers to identify the signs of dyslexia, it is most important to seek teaching strategies that will guide them through a successful learning process. There are cost-effective strategies that are easily implemented using accommodations to the existing curricula. According to Dr. Sally Shaywitz, author of *Overcoming Dyslexia* (2005), "dyslexia robs a person of time; accommodations return it" (Shaywitz, 2008, under Slow Readers Need More Time).

- Spelling. Do not focus on memorization. When doing written assignments, allow students to use computer software with spell check.
- Handwriting. Allow students to borrow notes from lessons. Record lessons using an audio or video device.
- Math. Allow students to use a calculator; always give choices when seeking oral responses.
- Written expression. Substitute drama, role-play, video presentations, murals, or computer presentations.
- Reading. Have audio books available and provide oral reading by peers.
- Homework. Shorten, assign, and collect. Be proactive with communication with parents.
- Test taking. Use a format such as matching the answer to the question by drawing a line. Give extended time, shorten the test, or use oral testing.

Avoid participation in spelling bees. Avoid individual oral reading or having the student write on the chalkboard. Allow these students to volunteer before calling on them to respond. Create a classroom that is a safe environment for mistakes. Nelson Rockefeller once said, "I was one of the 'puzzle children' myself—a dyslexic. . . . And I still have a hard time reading today. Accept the fact that you have a problem. Refuse to feel sorry for yourself. You have a challenge; never quit!"

3 Visual Communication Tools

When wrapping a gift, we are careful to cut only the amount of wrapping paper needed for the size of the gift; anything more is wasted. This is a good approach to consider when using photography. Think of the size of your photograph as the wrapping paper. Now consider your subject. Are you using all the wrapping paper, or have you wasted some?

If a student decides to communicate something about a tree in a photograph, he or she might fall into the all-too-common trap of backing up, then perfectly centering the entire tree. When viewing this photo, we find the top half of the picture to be beautiful blue sky, while the bottom half is wonderful green grass. And there, directly in the middle of the image, is the tree. Let us now reconsider the original intent of the student's communication: something about a tree. Place a transparency with a black tic-tac-toe style grid over the image. You should now see the photo evenly divided into nine equal squares. Each square represents a form of nonverbal communication. Compare this image to verbal communication and imagine this as a nine-word sentence. While reviewing the nine squares, we find the center square to be the only portion of the image that pertains to the tree. The remaining eight squares contain irrelevant information. We must now go back to our nine-word sentence and erase those eight words that were not used. By eliminating eight of nine words from a sentence, we are left with an incomplete thought—"tree"—that does not communicate. Therefore, this photo does not communicate its intended message. We ask the student to evaluate what he or she has learned and create a new photograph. This time, all nine squares should represent a portion of the communication. Once that is done, the message is concise and needs no interpretation.

There are differences between verbal and visual messages. Students need to understand how to read and interpret images, while increasing their awareness of the photographer's accountability for whatever formal and conceptual decisions are made in the process of creating a photograph. I recommend taking the communication one step farther by having the student turn the camera on an angle, or simply take a unique point of view, such as a bird's-eye view or a worm's-eye view. This approach still supports a full frame of communication, but now the communication or language becomes unique to that child. This is important because it stresses there can be no right or wrong. Appreciate the round-table effect this has in a classroom. Because each student is unique, there can be no mistakes (or miss-takes). Although two people might be observing the same subject, each brings something different to a photographic interpretation.

Photography is a language. Just like the written word, it has its own vocabulary and grammar. Effective imaging, like effective writing or speak-

ing, depends on understanding and applying some basic principles. Photography might be called an art of selection. The vocabulary a photographer works with is made up of the visual elements that exist all around us. Anything we see is by definition a visual element. The grammar of photography is the way in which visual elements are selected, isolated, related to other elements, or otherwise emphasized in a photograph. The choice of visual elements and their arrangement are the techniques a photographer uses to communicate an idea. "The process of making images and writing about pictures is powerful and revealing in a variety of contexts and settings. Providing children with an opportunity to master photography is to allow them access to expression" (Ewald, 2002, 163). We have something to say and we want to show it. Our subject is important. It is useful and critical information, but it is fragile until it is delivered. "Delivering information" is what we mean by "communicating."

The effectiveness of information delivery, or communication, falls along a spectrum that ranges from passive communication (when a visually important idea is obscured by an unorganized picture field, an excess of unrelated or unimportant visual elements, or conflicting and confusing information) to active communication (when there are interesting lines of continuity, dramatic colors, strong shapes, repeating patterns, and visual elements organized into a story). Communication channels as diverse as speech, the written word, and the photographic image all can be qualified in this way.

Most educators can readily identify the elements or conditions that make for ineffective or passive written communication. They also can identify the techniques that can help a student's writing become more powerful or active. In the world of photographic image making, there is a parallel set of techniques. Like mastering the skills of powerful writing, mastering the skills of photography can be a life's work, but learning and applying these techniques is relatively easy.

There is a strong connection between image and word—a natural resonance. Although the number of great writers who have also been visual artists may not be large, most writers would probably admit to having been moved and inspired by powerful images.

WHAT IS INFINITY?

I was once observing in a tenth-grade math class. The teacher was creative, enthusiastic, and had engaged most of her students. She was teaching the concept of infinity, which tends to be abstract at any age. She reminded the class of all the time and activities they had devoted to the concept of infinity throughout the course of the week. With ten minutes left in the period, she asked, "Who can tell me the definition of infinity?" No hands went up. Some students went into the always popular "I'm pretending to think, please don't call on me mode," while other students simply avoided making eye contact with the teacher. Then there was Gregory, seated in the front row, apparently for a reason. He had his head down on the desk with his hood pulled up as a shade for his slumber. When the teacher placed her hand on Gregory's shoulder, he popped up and blurted, "Infinity? I don't know what that is, but it might be like a round oatmeal box." With that the class broke into laughter and the teacher had to refocus her students with just moments left of class period. "Why is infinity like a round oatmeal box?" she asked. He replied that when he ate breakfast each morning he would look at the box. On the box was a picture of a man with long white hair and a black hat, a Quaker. In his hand was a box of oatmeal and on that small box was a small picture of a man holding a box of oatmeal. On that tiny box was a tiny picture of a man holding a box of oatmeal. As Gregory continued his definition, the teacher listened intently. Finally, Gregory paused. Looking at his teacher, he asked, "Do ya' get it?" Again, the room filled with laughter. With that, another student told how she could see forever by holding one mirror reflecting at an angle into another mirror. Here were two perfect definitions of infinity, yet minutes earlier, and after a week of instruction, not one hand went up to respond to the question, "What is infinity?" Why? Because as teachers we often forget there are two worlds of learning. The first world is "our world." It is our world in the sense that our tax money built it and supplied it, and we became certified to teach in it, inviting all students to come into our world to absorb as much as we have to give in what little time we have. However, there is indeed another world—"their world." That is the world beyond the boundaries of the school. Sometimes we find that what is being taught in our world may have already been learned in their world, yet we fail to bring the two worlds together, to build the bridge for our students. What finally did bring both worlds together was a photograph on a box of oatmeal that communicated to a teenage boy.

Photographic language is everywhere. When traveling sixty-five miles per hour down a freeway, we do not have much time to read printed information on a billboard. What must communicate to us is an image or photograph. We must glance up at the image and realize that by using that product we will look like the healthy person portrayed on the billboard. This information is communicated to us in seconds if the visual language is clear and concise.

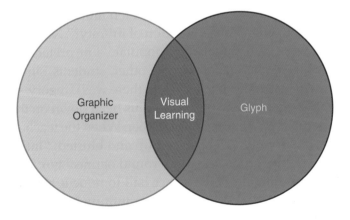

GRAPHIC ORGANIZERS

Graphic organizers are visual representations of knowledge, concepts, or ideas. Visual thinkers convert and compress information into an organized, easy-to-read graphic display. Like visual thinking maps and image mapping cards (see Chapter 6), graphic organizers are individualized yet generic templates that can be used with any subjects. Translating thought into a visual increases the likelihood of retention, promotes comprehension, clarifies information, and becomes a product of authentic assessment. Visuals can also be used to illustrate a student's prior knowledge on a given subject. According to *Graphic Organizers*, a review of research (Institute for the Advancement of Research in Education at Appalachia Educational Laboratory/ Advantia [IARE/AEL], 2003), graphic organizers use visual learning to improve student performance in critical thinking, retention, comprehension, and organization. Sometimes referred to as concept maps, mind maps, or entity relationship charts, graphic organizers may take on many forms:

- Relational organizers: Cause and effect webs, charts, and storyboards
- Category or classification organizers: Mind maps and concept mapping
- Sequence organizers: Cycles, chains, and ladders
- Compare-and-contrast organizers: Venn diagrams
- Concept development organizers: Flow chart, circle chart, word web, and story web

GLYPHS

A glyph is a symbol that conveys information nonverbally (Merriam-Webster, 2003, 534). Although glyphs are used in many ways, such as pictorial computer data, medical science, and dentistry, their origin dates back to picture writing ("hieroglyphics") that first appeared around 3000 BC (Coe, 1992). A glyph can be a displayed or printed image, as well as a single letter, mark, or ligature. Because of their use as a visual language, glyphs have many uses in the classroom of the visual teacher. Glyphs give students methods of arranging information into concepts based on characteristics that define an object or thought.

Glyphs can take the form of a graph. The graph can be used to show several different variables about a single subject. Glyphs combine the representation of data with visual art. They are nonstandard and can be used to illustrate a variety of information. Because glyphs are an innovative instrument that can reveal several pieces of information simultaneously, a legend must be generated in order to understand the nature of the visual language. A legend is the representational key, illustrating what each variable means.

When introducing students to glyphs, use role-play with some of the students to create a living glyph. Have six students stand in a row at the front of the classroom, facing the class. Ask another student to create the legend on the chalkboard or whiteboard, then ask the students questions for which they will respond with an action based on the legend. For example, "Who has completed their book report?" = Lift your right foot. "Who thinks last night's homework was difficult?" = Touch your hair. "Who thinks last night's homework was simple?" = Place your hands on your hips. The teacher should pose several similar questions. The seated students will then be asked to use the legend in order to answer questions based on the responses of the six students in front of the class. For example, "What percentage of the students thinks the homework was difficult?" requires the students to review the number of students who touched their hair. "What percentage of students thinks the homework was simple?" requires the students to review the number of students who had their hands on their hips.

The students have now been introduced to glyphs using role-play, modeling, and the construction of a visual language. They are ready to begin generating individual glyphs that correspond to the subject material being taught. This is an excellent way for students to understand the concept of visual data interpretation, particularly in the areas of math and science.

Activity

Give each student a sheet of paper with a large square in the center. This square represents the student's yard. Give the students the following prompts:

1. If you have a birthday this month, draw a tree in your yard.

2. Draw a flower for each year of your age.

3. Draw a bush for each brother you have and a lawn chair for each sister you have.

4. Put a white fence around your yard if you walk to school most mornings or a brown fence if you ride the bus.

5. Draw a picnic table if you bring your lunch to school or a barbeque grill if you purchase lunch.

6. Draw a sidewalk if you play a musical instrument.

7. Draw a lamppost if you have a dog and a swing if you have a cat.

The legend used for the glyph should be posted in front of the class. To practice visual data interpretation, students should try to guess which glyph belongs to which student.

THE THREE LEVELS OF VISUAL COMMUNICATION

LEVEL 1. Passive

Photographs are passive when an unorganized picture field, an excess of unrelated or unimportant visual elements, or conflicting and confusing visual information obscures a visually important idea. "Passive viewing is all about taking your sense of sight for granted" (Schaefer, 1995, p. 33). On the positive side, a passive image usually does not suffer from technical flaws, and the photographer has selected an important subject.

LEVEL 2. Neutral

In the neutral range of the communication spectrum, we meet our viewers halfway. Photographers achieve neutrality by filtering out unnecessary visual information with a change in point of view and by utilizing the picture field more effectively. The two most important techniques for neutral image making follow:

1. Fill your viewfinder with your subject. Get as close to your subject as your camera's focal distance will allow.

2. Keep your background simple or use your background to reinforce your subject. Before you take the photograph, check the background and foreground of your photograph for any unimportant or

confusing visual elements. If you find any, consider changing your point of view or repositioning your subject in front of a simpler background.

LEVEL 3. Active

As active photographers, we look for relationships between the visual elements selected for our image. We organize our visual elements by looking for interesting lines, dramatic colors, strong shapes, and repeating patterns. This organization leads the eye into and around a picture field. To activate your photographs, consider the following:

1. Look for leading lines. Try turning your camera on a diagonal, then look for lines that seem to lead one's eyes into the picture space or across it diagonally.

2. Find patterns. Look for visual elements that repeat to form patterns in your picture.

3. Pay attention to colors, textures, shapes, and forms. Are there strong color relationships in your picture? Are there strong shapes?

4. Tell a story with each image. Look for humor, mystery, suspense, and emotion. Keep an eye out for odd juxtapositions and contrasts.

DECODING

These three levels of visual communication outline helpful ways to become proficient in the encoding process. Opposite encoding is decoding—translating what the imagery is meant to communicate. Often a single image may have multiple meanings when decoded by more than one individual. I conducted an experiment with third graders to explore further the decoding element of visual communication. I asked each student to take a photograph of something that represents the word "happy" and something that represents the word "sad." Two students shot the same photograph of a bench in the schoolyard. The first student, Patrick, labeled his image of the bench "sad," while the second student, Sarah, labeled hers "happy." After the activity, I interviewed each student asking them why they chose that particular image and corresponding label. Patrick said he chose the image because he feels sad when the older students sit on that bench before school and throw rocks at him and his friends while they played on the schoolyard equipment. Sarah told me she feels happy when, two minutes before her recess period is supposed to end, the other third-grade class joins her class and the two teachers sit on the bench talking, losing track of the time, thereby allowing Sarah's class a double recess period.

Throughout this book, you will find unique images that are purposely placed with corresponding text. These images were selected to serve as individual exercises in the decoding process. After you have read the book, I invite you to use your new knowledge of visual handling skills and review each image. What do the images communicate when they are not in tandem with text? Do certain images carry more than one meaning? This exercise is particularly helpful in understanding the relevance of visual communication skills to everyday life. A similar activity might be to watch a movie for a second time without volume. What do the scenes communicate when not accompanied by spoken language and music? Do the scenes carry different meanings?

GENERAL PHOTO TIPS

Decide what your subject will be. Be sure the theme of your image is obvious.

Hold your camera steady, close to your body. This enables you to ensure inadvertent movement does not blur your image.

Decide between portrait and landscape. As a rule of thumb, hold your camera vertically when shooting portraits and horizontally when shooting landscapes. When it comes to creative photography, though, rules are made to be broken.

Fill your viewfinder with your subject. You have a limited amount of space to communicate your thoughts and ideas. Take advantage of that space by filling it with those images that will accurately convey your message.

Use flash indoors. Fluorescent lights cast a green-yellow tint and tungsten lights cast a red-yellow tint. Use the flash to bleach out the tints caused by indoor lighting.

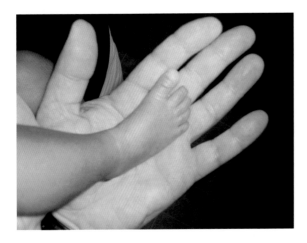

Use fill-in flash outdoors. Many cameras are now equipped with an automatic fill-in flash option. This feature allows you to lighten shadows cast from sunlight, and is especially useful when making images of people.

Keep your background simple or use your background to reinforce your subject. An abundance of extraneous information confuses the message being communicated. The message should be clear and concise, like a well-written sentence.

Look for leading lines. A leading line can be a road, path, sidewalk, fence, river, hedge, tree line, or shadow. Lines in a photograph should lead into, not out of, the image, and they should lead your eye toward your subject.

Change your point of view. Turn the camera to varying angles. Change the perspective of the subject by shooting at a downward or upward angle.

Find patterns. These might include abstract patterns or natural patterns, such as rows of trees or artificial patterns such as buildings. Pay attention to colors, textures, shapes, and forms.

Pay close attention to composition. A principle taught in graphic design and photography is the "Rule of Thirds," based on the theory that the eye goes naturally to a point about two-thirds up the page. By visually dividing the image into thirds, either vertically or horizontally, you achieve informal or asymmetric balance.

Give subjects something to do. One of the most common poses in photographs is the waist-up, perfectly centered, portrait, with subject looking directly into the camera. Images are far more interesting when the subject is allowed to be active.

Decide between wide angle and telephoto lenses. Most cameras are equipped with wide-angle lens by default. We often shoot images of people from a close range, which can distort the image somewhat. This is because the human eye has more of a "zoomed-in" and not a wide-angled view. It is better to step away from the subject and use the camera's zoom feature to come in tight for the photograph.

Shoot outside pictures in the morning or late afternoon. During these times, the sun's proximity to the earth provides much warmer hues and richer color tones. Shadows are more prominent and become creative contributions to the quality of the image.

Exhale prior to releasing the shutter. Basketball players are taught to exhale just prior to releasing the ball. This strategy helps to ensure stability in the hands of the player, thereby increasing the likelihood of success. This technique also helps to ensure camera stability, thereby increasing the likelihood the image will not be blurry.

Tell a story with each image. The better one communicates with an image, the more that image tells a story. What happened just before the shutter was released? What will happen just after the shutter is released?

Don't be afraid to experiment. Some of the most memorable images come from accidents. Renowned photographer John Schaefer tells the story of shooting several images of artist Waldo Midgley (1888–1983). Each image seemed to lack the magic Schaefer typically looked for in the composition of his images. Then, without warning, just prior to the final click of his shutter, Midgley's pet cat jumped into the camera's frame, providing the perfect balance needed for Schaefer's mind's eye. Fascinating images can come from creative experimentation—and accidents. Enjoy the photographs that both of these methods can give you.

DIGITAL PHOTO TIPS

Digital photography has found its way into our pockets, cell phones, and even our computers. Here are some overall tips specific to the digital form of imagery, with particular regard to hand-held cameras.

Don't be too hasty to erase. What you may consider an undesirable photograph at a given moment may have an interesting appeal later. A photograph can always be erased. Take a second look later in a day, and then make your decision.

Take pictures through the viewfinder and not by looking at the LCD screen. The LCD (liquid crystal display) screen should be used only to review an image. It drains battery power. The camera's viewfinder is designed to assist you in the composition of your photograph.

Take extra batteries with you at all times. Many digital cameras have rechargeable batteries. When using the LCD screen or video-capable cameras, the batteries lose power quickly. To save battery power try

- switching off the flash;
- not using the LCD screen;
- turning off button beeps and sound effects;
- using a card reader to transfer images to a computer, as opposed to connecting directly to the camera; and
- using high drain rechargeable batteries such as NiMH 2300mAh. Standard AA disposable batteries do not last as long.

Use the flash override for portraits. Digital cameras do an excellent job of reading existing light. Using the flash to shoot portraits of people often bleaches detail and facial features, due to the proximity of the camera to the subject.

Take lots of pictures. Since your images are digitally recorded onto a storage device, you are not wasting film. Take full advantage of your storage capacity.

Consider a digital photograph as a starting point. Most digital cameras come with proprietary software programs that enable you to sharpen, darken, lighten, crop, contrast, and perform many other artistic steps. Programs that are more extensive can be found in third-party software. Although pricey, Adobe's Photoshop tends to be the industry's standard.

Decide whether to use an inkjet printer. Inkjet printers tend to print darker images that can be overly saturated with color. This is because the image file is an RGB (red-green-blue). To improve color reproduction, convert the file to a CMYB (cyan-magenta-yellow-black) using applications such as Photoshop and Paint Shop Pro.

Carry plenty of storage media. Most digital cameras come equipped with storage devices such as discs and various memory-card formats, including Smart

Media, Compact Flash, xD, MS, SD, and MMC. These devices also come in different storage capacities.

TECHNOLOGY-BASED INSTRUCTION

Digital technology may be transforming definitions of literacy for the masses, and the shift may indeed favor visual intelligence. Visual vocabulary is undervalued in education, and there is a need for collaboration between those in the visual and verbal arts.

—Dyc & Milligan (2000)

There are essentially two ways of creating digital images. You can begin with a traditional photographic image and digitize it with a scanner, or you can record an image with a digital camera.

Whichever method you choose, you will need to make two choices in fairly short order. You will need to select a level of image resolution, sometimes called PPI (pixels per inch), and you will need to decide on a file format (TIFF, JPEG, GIF, etc.).

All photographs are made up of dots. Traditional photographs are optical illusions generated by clumping specks of silver halide or light-sensitive color dyes. Look at any photograph closely and you will see a pattern of dots; photographers call this grain. Digital images are also made up of dots, but instead of random granulation, these dots are made up of the smallest unit a screen can display as black, white, or some color. This unit is called a *pixel*. The abbreviation PPI (not to be confused with DPI, or dots per inch) refers to the number of pixels per inch in the image.

When you make an image on film, you do not have to choose the resolution. (Technically, though, you do have some control over this. The higher the ISO rating of a roll of film, the more apparent is the grain you will see when you enlarge an image.) When you scan an image or use a digital camera to record your image, you need to select a resolution. This is not as difficult as it sounds. The resolution at which you should scan or record an image depends on two points: the end use of the image, and the capacity of your computer to work with and store these large files.

The higher the resolution at which you scan the image (the higher the number of pixels per inch sampled), the sharper and more accurate the image will appear. This is a general rule of thumb: high resolution = high level of image fidelity = large file size.

Three Rules for Working with Digital Images

1. You can make pictures smaller than the size at which you scanned or recorded them, but you cannot make them bigger.

Well, okay, you *can* make them bigger. That is, your software will allow you to do it, but you lose a significant amount of image quality when you do. To make an image larger, your software has to add pixels. It will do this by guessing what color pixel to add, based on the color of the pixels on either side of where it is adding them. This is called interpolation. It sounds like a good idea, but the results are usually disappointing. It is your computer's best guess at what those pixels might look like given the surrounding pixels.

2. Manipulate your images first.

Saving an image as a JPEG file for the Internet is a form of compressing it. This way it will take up less space and move more quickly through cyberspace. It will also download and open faster and take less room on your hard drive. Compression schemes always result in a reduction of image quality, but the trade-off is often worth it. Manipulating your photos (using Photoshop, Photo Deluxe, or some other image-editing program) on the uncompressed file means you have more raw picture data to work with. After you have made your changes, compress the file to a JPEG or similar format.

3. Identify the end-use of your image before you digitize it.

In general, scan or create images at twice the DPI required for your end-use. This allows you to manipulate the image first and then compress it.

Photograph for Web Sites

1. Scan black-and-white images in grayscale (eight bit) instead of bitmap (two bit) mode. This will allow you more latitude in fine-tuning the image for best display on computer screens.

2. Scanning black-and-white or color images of a resolution of at least 144 PPI allows you to resize, sharpen, edit, adjust color balance, and improve contrast with more control.

3. For most images going straight to Web sites, scanning at 72 PPI is the standard. Many monitors cannot show a higher resolution.

Print Publication

For most print publications, scanning at 300 PPI is a workable compromise that will give you acceptable image quality with manageable image files. You probably still will want to save these image files off your main system. It does not take many images to fill up that system.

File Format Types

TIFF (tagged image file format). Best file format for working with images that will be printed out later. This format supports high-resolution display but creates big file sizes. It is a common file format and most imaging programs support it. It also converts easily to other formats.

GIF (graphics interchange format). Good format for in-line icons, clip art, and other low-resolution graphics. Not great for photographs where resolution and detail matter.

JPEG (joint photographic experts group). Best file format for photographs on Web pages. It displays images rapidly and at good resolution due to its compression format.

USING THE INTERNET IN THE CLASSROOM

Using the Internet in the schools is critical to shrinking the digital divide. Sixty-eight percent of low-income families rely on schools for Internet access (National School Board Association, 2008). It is the responsibility of our school system to focus on two priorities with regard to effective Internet use: keeping students safe and increasing student achievement. According to a recent study conducted by the Grunwald Associates (2008), 70 percent of students use the Internet at home, 56 percent use the Internet at school, including preschool, 9 percent use the Internet at a friend's or relative's home, and 6 percent use the Internet at a public library.

The National School Board Association used the Grunwald research to suggest guidelines to educational leaders and parents on student use of the Internet.

- Schools should work with parents as a community to develop strategic guidelines on school and home Internet use. The harmony will keep a necessary balance as opposed to a one-sided imposition of rules.
- Schools should focus equal attention on accessing good content and restricting bad content. Overzealous district policies could create unwanted obstacles to the educational value of the Internet.
- Schools should develop and implement a formal plan designed to help the schools and parents teach safe, responsible uses of the Internet. This might include keeping family computers in shared rooms in the home. In addition, both learning environments should emphasize that students should never share personal information.
- Schools should include preschoolers in learning about the Internet. The Internet is a wonderful opportunity to begin building early skills required for literacy and cognitive learning.
- Schools should provide continuing resources for parents, such as educationally related Web sites or electronic forums to bring the community into the learning process.
- Schools should not assume that people who own computers are computer savvy. As a community, we need to offer classes to instruct on the use of the computer and Internet training. With concerted effort, this can be coordinated through libraries, community centers, and local colleges and universities.

MEDIA LITERACY

According to the Public
Broadcasting Service Teacher Source

- Sixty-five percent of American children have television sets in their bedrooms
- The average seventh-grader watches three hours of TV each day
- Excessive TV viewing has been linked to obesity
- On average, U.S. children who have video games at home play with them ninety minutes a day
- Eighty-nine percent of school-age kids own video game equipment
- By the age of eighteen, the average U.S. child's TV viewing has included sixteen thousand murders
- In the top twenty TV shows among teen viewers in 2001–02, the average number of scenes per hour with sexual content is 6.7
- According to a 2002 poll, the average American teen asked his or her parents nine times for products seen advertised before the parent eventually agreed to purchase the item
- The federal Children's Television Act of 1990 and its update in 1996 require television broadcasters to air only three hours of educational children's programming per week
- By the time kids are senior citizens, they will have spent three years of their lives watching commercials
- Forty percent of American families "almost always" watch TV while eating dinner
- Twenty-three percent of Americans under the age of thirty read the newspaper on a typical day

The Center for Media Literacy defines Media Literacy as a "21st century approach to education. It provides a framework to access, analyze, evaluate, and create messages in a variety of forms—from print to video to the Internet. Media literacy builds an understanding of the role of media in society as well as essential skills of inquiry and self-expression necessary for citizens of a democracy" (Center for Media Literacy, n.d.). As a nation, we are beginning to realize that more and more Americans are getting their information from television and not from books and newspapers. According to a Kaiser Foundation study (Kaiser Foundation, 2005), today's youth spend the equivalent of a full workweek (about forty hours) using media each week. As a result, it is imperative that our youth recognize how media influence and manipulate. They must utilize critical thinking about the messages in media and uncover subliminal information and the exploration of values. They should possess the ability to interpret media accurately, thereby avoiding any potential damage to their self-esteem. This can be accomplished through media education.

Parents and teachers should seek resources and develop ways to empower youth to think critically and understand the behind-the-scenes production of what they are viewing. They need to understand how to analyze sound and imagery for what it is, and not for what it appears to be. We live in a world of technology, a world of television, movies, music, and advertising. Teaching media education at a young age helps children grasp issues of values, popular culture, faith development, justice and social issues, and spirituality. It empowers our youth and ultimately strengthens our society's democratic structures. It is a lifelong process of active and participatory investigative learning.

Research shows that learning math from computer games that use multiple representations is superior to learning from those using only one. However, there is also research revealing that computer learning as an isolated method with these programs is not sufficient. Students need verbal support or direction when using multimedia programs for learning to absorb fully the best long-term comprehension of skills. For several students, multimedia programs are very unproductive for learning math processes. Students with very limited understanding of computer use and students with poor working memory would benefit more from alternative pedagogical methods. This research shows that verbal guidance paired with discovery-based computer programs gives the optimal results for learning complex arithmetic systems in many, but not all, students (Moreno & Duran, 2004). Since the 1960s, we have recognized the importance of media literacy. Research, education, and resources are now only a mouse-click away.

Encourage critical thinking skills. Students should analyze all forms of media messages, and should be taught to understand that these messages might be interpreted in different ways based on an individual's background and culture. Discuss media with your students. Ask them to look for particular details prior to reading or viewing videos, then ask them questions about what they have read or seen. Highlight the various ways commercial media infringe on other types of media content. Today's student is bombarded with media. This can be used to your advantage. Use video clips from favorite movies or daily shows to generate interest in a new topic.

Have students create a video montage to illustrate an opinion or a specific subject. Challenge them to explore all types of media, looking for commonalities and subliminal messages. This is their world, the world beyond the boundaries of the school building. By understanding their world, teachers can more effectively convey classroom information by utilizing a variety of instructional media sources (books, newspapers, magazines, videos, and the Internet). While using these materials, students will become more aware of current events. However, be sure to instruct them on the issues of credibility and bias in the media. Good information comes from many sources. One method used to illustrate this concept is to have students compare a corporate Web site to that of a nonprofit organization. They will see how diverse stories and representations can emerge through the Internet. Another idea is to ask students to keep a television-viewing log detailing gender role stereotypes in media programming. Use this log to document the portrayal of violence, whether in dramas or in sitcoms.

Five Key Questions of Media Literacy

When teaching media literacy, expose the students to the five key questions of media literacy. These questions assist students in mastering the skill of understanding the nature of communications, particularly with regard to telecommunications and mass media. They will gain knowledge of the structural attributes of the media, and, most importantly, how these attributes might influence the content of the media.

1. Who created this message?

2. What creative techniques are used to attract my attention?

3. How might different people understand this message differently from me?

4. What values, lifestyles, and points of view are represented in or omitted from this message?

5. What is the message being sent?

Remember, "media literacy" is the outcome of instruction. Let students know that people in movies, sitcoms, and commercials are not real—they are actors. Screenwriters and directors dictate their vocabulary. If your students see a commercial portraying a "blue-collar worker" and the actor uses the word "ain't," it does not mean that blue-collar workers are intellectually "less than," it means the director made a conscious decision to bias the viewer's opinion of blue-collar workers.

Classroom Suggestions

Language Arts

- Use media to document and store memories.
- Compare a movie to the book on which it was based.
- Define what advertising is and when or why something is not considered an advertisement.
- Evaluate Web sites.
- Evaluate the credibility of information sources.

Fine Arts

- Who's renting your eyeballs? Analyze the use of visual arts in advertising by exploring the ten techniques of persuasion.
  - Humor
  - Macho
  - Friends
  - Family
  - Fun
  - Nature
  - Sexy
  - Cartoon
  - Celebrity
  - Wealth

- Analyze the use of performing arts in advertising.
- Analyze music videos.
- Investigate the design elements of political cartoons.
- Analyze imagery in newspapers and world news Web sites.
- Explore how artists are portrayed, particularly in movies and television.

Math

- Use media to develop categorization skills.
- Guide students in the discovery that the same set of data can be represented differently in order to emphasize a particular message, especially in political advertisements.
- Explore the ratio of advertisement to news in newspapers, magazines, Web sites, television, and radio.
- Build problem-solving skills by scrutinizing syllogisms and hypothetical reasoning through advertising.

Science

- Conduct experiments on advertised products to verify the validity of the advertisement.
- Investigate medical research claims used to sell products.
- Explore how scientists are portrayed in movies and television.
- Study how natural disasters are portrayed in the media.
- Pose the question, "Does the media assist in the study of science? If so, how?"

Social Studies

- Investigate the relationship between media and terrorism.
- Examine the television advertising strategies of the 2008 presidential election.
- Produce a video or multimedia presentation based on a thematic unit.
- Have students keep a log of their families' media consumption for one week.
- Ask students how they think foreigners perceive American media.

Health

- Examine how mass media advertising attempts to solve health-related problems.
- Have students document the number of sexual content incidents in a primetime television program.
- Discuss how families and ethnic groups are portrayed in television programs and advertising.
- Discuss whether gender bias in advertising targets children.
- Examine how women's bodies are portrayed in advertising.
- Discuss what techniques are used in ads that popularize pharmaceutical products.
- Examine food labels for buzz phrases like "low-carb," "all natural," or "highly recommended."

Early Childhood

- Have students keep a log of how much time they spend in front of a television in a seven-day period.
- Regardless of what age you are influencing, teach the dos and don'ts of using the Internet.

With the influx of technology, visual learning and media literacy are perhaps more critical than they have been at any other time in history. It is essential for teachers to explore the world of technology, where their students reside, in order to teach the way the students are learning.

Video. Record classroom presentations and lessons during instruction. Guide students to integrate video into their school projects. This provides an effective way to personalize the work and provide ownership, while promoting enjoyment and motivation.

Video gaming. Video gaming is often frowned on by parents and educators as addictive electronics that come between study habits and healthy physical activity. Again, we must find the balance between keeping students from harm's way and researching the educational benefits of video gaming. According to Doug Lowenstein, president of the Entertainment Software Association, "sixty-five percent of American heads of households play computer and video games. The average game player is thirty-five years old and has been playing games for twelve years" (Entertainment Software Association, 2008). The theory maintains that video gaming can teach skills such as analytical thinking, multitasking, and problem solving under duress. According to Don Blake, a technology analyst for the National Education Association, making the leap to educational video gaming has enormous potential. In fact, Austin, Texas, video gaming company, Aspyr Media Inc., is partnering with Kaplan Inc., a New York–based company dedicated to helping individuals achieve their educational goals. Together, these companies will create a Scholastic Aptitude Test (SAT) prep video game for the popular Nintendo DS hand-held game console (Omar Gallaga, "Austin's Aspyr to bring SAT prep to Nintendo *DS*," *Austin* [Texas] *American-Statesman*).

Downloadable TV. There are free applications, such as Miro, that can be downloaded to Windows-, Mac-, or Linux-driven computers. These applications can convert your computer into an Internet video player. Many of the Internet channels are devoted to nature, science, history, space, tutorials, and newscasts from stations throughout the world.

Streaming multimedia. Streaming multimedia is constantly received by and normally displayed to the end-user while it is being delivered by the provider. Incorporating streaming video into the curriculum is a cutting-edge way to access educational programming and provide lectures and study tools to students anytime, anywhere. Video streaming content is real time, always current and up-to-date, and is widely available. Integrating this form of technology into a lesson catches students' attention and keeps them focused.

YouTube. This is a video-sharing service that lets users upload files to YouTube servers, where they are available online. Since its debut in 2005, YouTube has become extremely popular, streaming more than 100 million video clips a day. Students can experience creating educational video and can view videos, all while in conversation with commentators and creators. These activities utilize technology as a means of enhancing visual literacy, which is particularly important in our current electronic culture.

Google. This is an online and mobile advertising company offering Internet search, Web-based e-mail, online mapping, office productivity, social networking, and video sharing. Google offers educational discussion groups, activities created by educators, an educational blog entitled, "The Infinite Thinking Machine," and Google Earth, which combines the power of Google Search with satellite imagery, maps, terrain, and 3D buildings to put the world's geographic information at your fingertips. Google also offers SketchUp, a drawing program that enables users to draw three-dimensional objects. By using their program Picasa, users are able to import images to both SketchUp and Google Earth.

In summary, students should be aware of the importance of balancing and managing their individual and familial media diet. They should practice the art of analysis, scrutinizing what passes before their eyes, digging deeper into the political, social, and economic implications. Mass media are molding the lives of our young people much more than print. We must take an assertive stance in helping students decode imagery, particularly when it comes to telecommunications. The result will be a more proactive and comprehensive approach to our traditional teaching and learning system.

4 Fine Arts

If students aren't taught the language of sound and images, shouldn't they be considered as illiterate as if they left college without being able to read and write?

—George Lucas, filmmaker (*Edutopia,* 2004)

Making a schoolroom too quiet is a common mistake. Extremely quiet rooms can produce a feeling of sensory deprivation. Music, on the other hand, can soothe emotions and excite enthusiasm, while giving students a sense of cultural identity.

New studies suggest that playing music—and even just listening to it—may improve learning, memory, logic, and general creativity. Plato once said, "Music is a more potent instrument than any other for education." As with visuals, music is a terrific carrier of meaning, and is readily available for learning. The research describing the Mozart Effect tells us that music may be a powerful way to build reasoning, memory, and intelligence. Music can be used as a mood enhancer to get learners ready to learn. Music activates emotions and long-term memory and fully engages the brain's most receptive states. The brain is naturally designed to optimize all the senses. Combining visual learning and music creates a powerful synergy because it helps to regulate the brain's rhythm, which balances the specialized powers of the left and right hemispheres.

Is the human mind naturally wired for music? University of Toronto psychologist Sandra Trehub thinks so. In a test conducted in 2000, she varied the pitch, tempo, and melodic contour of music and found that babies detected changes in all three. Beyond Trehub's work, other research suggests that people typically can remember multiple tunes and melody-laden lyrics, and yet are limited in their recall of poetic passages.

The new studies on music and learning are in part attributed to an expanding level of research on the development of the human brain. Children are born with 100 billion unconnected neurons, or nerve cells, according to these studies. Occurrences such as seeing a mother's smile or hearing a mother or father speak, build connections between those nerve cells. Pathways in the brain that are not used ultimately fade. Therefore, a child's early experiences can help establish what that child will be like in adulthood. Dr. Anne Blood, a researcher at Massachusetts General Hospital, notes, "because [music] activates the parts of the brain that makes us happy it suggests that music benefits our physical and mental well-being" (National Academy of Sciences, 2001).

Just as the brain produces visual images, it also composes music. The Mozart Effect, a study that began in the 1990s, fed the brain's electrical patterns into a musical synthesizer. The results were recognizable patterns of music—some sounding Baroque, some like Eastern music, others like folk music. In other words, the neurons (nerve cells) "play music," similar to how the envisioning and communication processes are brought to life through photography.

An elementary principal in Higgens Lake, Michigan, "Dr. Jones," is a firm believer in the presence of the arts in the schools. Despite her protests, the district eliminated the art and music programs indefinitely. Budget cuts or no budget cuts, this principal was on a mission. She has part-time art and music teachers that instruct the students, one class session every two weeks. Although she feels this is "at best" inadequate, Dr. Jones makes do by ensuring original artwork is always on display and rotated throughout the school. Musical recitals are performed during in-school assemblies and evening performances for families a minimum of four times a year. She does everything in her power to make sure that every subject includes the arts within the current school-budget parameters. Her faculty takes part in visual learning professional development and incorporates the visual teaching methods and brain-compatible strategies into their curricula.

While on a visit to the Detroit Institute of Arts, Dr. Jones noticed a selection of discounted fine-art calendars from previous years. She bought all of them, cut apart all of the full-colored art replicas, and hung them throughout the school. She even displays them on the inside of the stalls in the lavatories. She rotates the prints monthly. This art has become a visual representation of a history that her students were no longer exposed to in formal instruction. She began playing classical music at low, soothing levels in the hallways and cafeteria via the school's intercom system. By adding visual cues coupled with music played at lower tempos, her students are consistently exposed to the visual arts. Initially the students complained about the "elevator music," but thought the pictures were "cool." As time passed, when the music was turned off to avoid sating the students, they asked for their music back. What was once victim to budgetary constraints now fills the eyes and ears of every student in the school. Visual information, coupled with music, appeals to the varying learning modalities and multiple intelligences. With the help of the masters and composers, Principal Jones was able to build mental bridges, while emphasizing the importance of fine arts in her school.

VISUAL MUSIC

In 1981, MTV (music television) launched an influential American cable network specializing in music-related programming. Top-forty music was no longer left to the imagination. It was no longer necessary to close our eyes and visualize the characters in the songs. Suddenly, bands and performers were in our living rooms singing directly to us, leaving nothing to the imagination. Video games were accompanied by heart-pounding music, designed to increase the flow of adrenaline while enhancing the visual impact of the game. To realize fully how music enhances visual perception, try watching a movie for the second time without any volume. Notice how drastically the dynamics of the visuals are altered. The emotional impact is removed, thereby defining the purpose of combining audio and visual. Music has a subliminal effect on us as well. Notice how calming the music is in high-stress environments, such as the dentist's or doctor's office. Notice how festive the music is in department stores, making us feel happy and much freer with our money. Notice the music in an elevator that subliminally takes the anxiety off the reality of our situation: that we are standing in a windowless box dangling from a cable while plummeting thirty stories at a high rate of speed.

Music has a power that can be harnessed and used effectively, especially in an educational environment. The key is to integrate music and visual learning in order to take full advantage of its positive effects.

THE SIX METHODS OF VISUAL/MUSICAL LEARNING

1. Investigating

Visual. Using images to learn about and better understand the world.

Musical. Various styles of music evoke various styles of learning. Music has built-in peaks and valleys, engaging fantasy and emotion, creating anticipation or excitement.

2. Chronicling

Visual. Freezing moments in time through documentation.

Musical. A song on the radio can bring back special memories.

3. Expressing

Visual. Using images to reveal thoughts and feelings, translating the abstract to the concrete.

Musical. The Mozart Effect demonstrates that music may be a powerful way to build reasoning, memory, and intelligence. Different tempos create different learning environments and different physical states (e.g., relaxation or excitement).

4. Communicating

Visual. Using images to share information with others.

Musical. Musical soundtracks are used to enhance sadness, joy, fear, and love, etc. To better understand their impact, try watching a movie with the volume off.

5. Inspiring

Visual. Using images to express and communicate to change behavior or attitude.

Musical. Music influences the rhythm of the heartbeat; affects physical energy with changes in metabolism; relieves fatigue and low energy; and stimulates creativity, sensitivity, and thinking.

6. Envisioning

Visual. Using images to encourage new connections and relationships.

Musical. Many of us learned the alphabet through flashcards or visual symbols. How many of us had to refer to the melody of "Twinkle, Twinkle, Little Star" before we actually mastered it? Refer to Chapter 6 of this book, Activities 235–247. They are designed to assist in making the connection between the power of music and visual communication.

AFFECTING THE BRAIN WITH COLOR

As educators, we are trained to recognize the differences between hearing and listening. Much can be said about the idiom of "in one ear and out the other." The classroom that relies strictly on the spoken word will invariably fall short in the impact of a dynamic model lesson.

There is a significant difference between looking and seeing. The human eye is often too comfortable and unconsciously conforms to its view and moves on, not bothering to probe and process the visual information. *Looking* is a passive use of vision. Looking makes no demands on the brain. It can be taken for granted, similar to the way one regards respiration and heart rhythm. This is due in part to the modernization of our lifestyles made possible by the absence of physical threat. Unlike prehistoric people, modern men and women strive and are able to alleviate threats or anxiety. We effectively accomplish this by making daily schedules and clear expectations for ourselves. Daily patterns and routines satisfy our overall need for safety. We are not required to think about them. We pass the same trees and bushes in our front yard several times a day. We look at them, but do not see them. Our vision tends to be taken for granted as we go about our mundane, day-to-day tasks. *Seeing*, on the other hand, requires both sensory input and mental scrutiny. It leaves indelible marks on one's mind, and requires discovery. Discovery leads to interpretation and understanding. Understanding forms the building blocks of learning.

No one can deny that color has been both a necessity and a luxury in our fundamental existence. The origin of color's significance is best described by the translated and edited version of the *Luscher Color Test* (Luscher, 1948/1969), translated by Ian A. Scott. The book is based on Dr. Max Luscher's 1948 studies:

> In the beginning man's life was dictated by two factors beyond his control: night and day, darkness and light. Night brought about an environment in which action had to cease, so man prepared his cave, wrapped himself in furs and went to sleep, or else he climbed a tree and made himself as comfortable as he could while awaiting the coming of dawn. Day brought an environment in which action was possible. So he set forth once more to replenish his store and forage or hunt for his food. Night brought passivity, quiescence and a general slowing down of metabolic and glandular activity; day brought with it the probability of action, an increase in the metabolic rate and greater glandular secretion, thus providing him with both energy and incentive. (p. 86)

Color is light, and light is energy. The emotional impacts that colors have on our brains are easier to understand if viewed through the lens of the survival associations required by primitive man. Color meanings have evolved through the centuries, but they stem from prehistoric visual needs. However, culture, religion, technology, and geographic location also have affected the meaning of color through history.

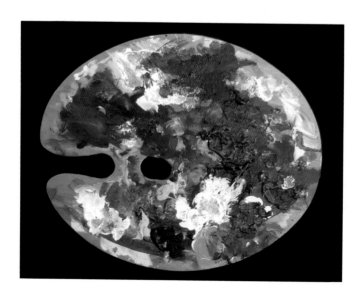

The Meaning of Color Through the Ages

	Color impact on primitive people (Luscher, 1948/1969)	Color impact during the Middle Ages in Europe (Edwards, 1999)	Color impact on people today (Hewlett-Packard, 1999)
Red	excitement, attack	courage, zeal	energy, optimism, passion, dynamism, intensity, danger
Orange	strength	strength, endurance	joy, courage, ambition, fun, balance, organism, warmth
Yellow	hope, activity		enthusiasm, playfulness, optimism, joy, action, hope, sunshine
Green	food	youth, fertility	generosity, nature, envy, hope, fertility, good luck, success
Light Blue	coolness, calmness		quiet, coolness, calmness, softness, purity, understanding, peace
Dark Blue	quiet, passivity	purity, sincerity	tranquility, intuition, trustworthiness, peace, harmony, security
Purple		royalty, high birth	spirituality, royalty, mystery, wisdom, independence, wealth
Pink			friendliness, love, compassion, sweetness, faithfulness, softness
Gold		honor	illumination, wisdom, wealth
Brown	restfulness, neutrality	commonness	stability, reliability, comfort, masculinity, simplicity, earthiness
Black		grief, penitence	
White		fate, purity	
Grey	free from stimulus, no-man's land		

Global Significance of Color

Red	China: good luck India: purity Eastern cultures: signifies joy when combined with white
Orange	Ireland: religious significance (Protestant)
Yellow	Asia: sacred, imperial
Green	China and France: negative significance for package goods India: color of Islam
Dark Blue	China: immortality Hindus: color of Krishna, dusk
Pastels	Korea: trust
Brown	Colombia: discourages souls

Certain colors have an enormous influence over our perceptions of daily life and on our behavior. For example, the warm tones of red stimulate the senses and raise the blood pressure, while blue calms and relaxes. The visual effect of color on its surroundings is often communicated in nature. Many male birds are brightly colored, thus attracting the female's attention. The chameleon eliminates possible danger by changing its skin color to match its environment.

Color affects the space in which we live. Color is continuously altered by the ever-changing angle of the sun. The amount of light entering our visual cortex influences our perception of color. The light from the sun affects how we perceive color. The sea appears blue under a blue sky and gray under a gray sky because water appears to be the color of the light that illuminates it. In essence, color is visual magic. Every day we make a choice in color harmony based on the clothing we choose to wear. Color choices are an integral part of our lifestyle, including the foods we eat, drawing colored lines on a bar graph, planting a flowerbed, or wrapping a gift. By increasing our knowledge of color and how it changes us emotionally and physically, we increase our visual pleasure in the world of seeing.

How does color affect us physiologically and psychologically? The psychological effects of a color are often more meaningful than the visual experience. Pantone, Inc., known as the standard language for color communication for more than forty years, reported that an executive for a paint company received complaints from workers in a blue office that the office was too cold. When the offices were painted a warm peach, the sweaters came off even though the temperature had not changed. Businesses tend to take advantage of the emotional triggers that color has on the mind and body. The use of the color red in fast food restaurants is not accidental. Studies indicate that red interiors increase one's appetite. According to Pantone's article on the psychology of color, "People will actually gamble more and make riskier bets when seated under a red light as opposed to a blue light. That is why Las Vegas, Nevada, is the city of red neon" (Pantone 2008). Hues that approach red have almost universally been considered as warm colors, and those that tend toward blue as cool. Fire and sunlight and the glow of the brisk circulation of blood are all associated with warmth. The colors of the sky and distant mountains and cool waters are generally bluish. When the body is chilled, its color tends toward a bluish hue. These reasons naturally make us associate red, orange, and yellow with warmth, and blue, blue-green, and blue-violet with coolness.

One of the most interesting examples of color effects is Baker-Miller pink, a color that is similar to bubble-gum pink, also known as drunk tank pink. This color is used to calm violent prisoners in jails. Dr. Alexander Schauss, PhD, director of the American Institute for Biosocial Research in Tacoma, Washington, was the first to report the suppression of angry, antagonistic, and anxiety-ridden behavior among prisoners. "Even if a person tries to be angry or aggressive in the presence of pink, he can't. The heart muscles can't race fast enough. It's a tranquilizing color that saps your energy. Even the color-blind are tranquilized by pink rooms" (Walker, 1991, pp. 50–52; see also Morton, n.d.). In spite of these powerful effects, there is substantial evidence that these reactions are short term. Once the body returns to a state of equilibrium, a prisoner may regress to an even more agitated state. According to a 1991 article in the *Honolulu Star Bulletin* (Morton, 1991, pp. 50–52) University of Hawaii assistant coach George Lumkin noticed that the visitor locker rooms at the University of Iowa and at Colorado State University were painted pink, either the Baker-Miller variety or some similar hue, in order to calm the visiting teams' demeanors. Lumkin became angry, or as close to angry as one can get while in a pink room, and he complained. Thereafter, the Western Athletic Conference implemented a rule stating that the visiting teams' locker room cannot be painted a different color from the home teams' locker rooms.

Color is the visual information by which the eye perceives its surroundings. There are three primary colors: red, blue, and yellow. All other colors are made from these three colors. Secondary colors are the colors created when two colors are mixed, tertiary colors are the colors created when three colors are mixed, and so on.

We need sufficient light to perceive colors in our brain. Color is produced from light. Light is energy. The healthy human eye detects colors using six to seven million cones.

Cones are the conical photosensitive receptor cells of the vertebrate retina. The 120 million rods are more sensitive and numerous. A rod is the

long, rod-shaped photosensitive receptor in the retina responsive to faint light. Rods are used to distinguish black, gray, and white. They are very sensitive to movement and are extremely important when it comes to night vision.

A general conclusion of the stereotypical pirate's patch–covered eye is that his eye was injured and that the patch protected or hid his eye. Actually, the same pirate would be found covering the opposite eye in the evening using the same patch. This was a way for sailors to strengthen the rods' acuity for increased night vision on the open sea. Similarly, the United States Navy often requires the night guard to start the work shift by sitting in a light-tight room for at least thirty minutes prior to duty, thereby preparing the sailor for optimal vision in a starlit sky.

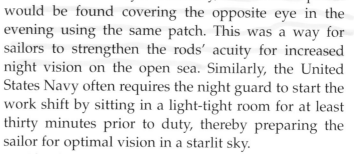

The discovery of the structure of color came from a scientific perspective thanks to mathematician and physicist Sir Isaac Newton. A century later, German poet and scholar Johann Wolfgang von Goethe began studying the psychological effect of colors through a more artistic perspective. The need for the brain to create harmonious balance can be found in the placement order of colors on the color wheel. To show the effect primary colors have on the cones, the eyes must first be fatigued. To cause what is known as an after-image in the visual cortex, try staring at the dot in the center of the red circle for approximately forty-five to sixty seconds. Try not to blink. At the end of the time, quickly shift your eyes to the blank, white area below the red circle. You should instantly see green, the complementary color of red, on the white surface. Eventually, this after-image will trail off the pages and disappear. This experiment to find the color balance can be done with any color on the color wheel. The after-image will always be the color that is opposite on the wheel. Color opposites attract by producing vibrating, electrical stimuli in our mind's eye. To illustrate color illusions that take place in the brain, take two identical colors and surround them by different backgrounds. Notice how different they appear to be, even though they are the same. When you perceive a colored object, your brain determines its color in the context of the surrounding colors and lighting effects. This sensation or translation of color is unique to each individual and as varied as the taste receptors on our palettes, or the preferential olfactory sensations.

Colors affect our actions and reactions in traffic as well as in interior environments such as classrooms. Colors can create conditions that cause fatigue, increase stress, decrease visual perception, damage eyesight, increase possible errors, and negatively affect orientation and safety. Colors can also create positive and productive conditions: Blue and green are calming. Brighter colors such as red, orange, and yellow tend to be exciting and energetic. Most teachers prefer lighter colors, which induce positive feelings in the classroom. Try to avoid white; many consider it a disturbing or disruptive color. According to researchers, color visuals increase willingness to read, motivation, and participation by up to 80 percent (Green, 1984). Color enhances learning and improves retention by more than 75 percent (Hewlett-Packard, 1999). Color accounts for 60 percent of the acceptance or rejection of an object and is a critical factor in the success of any visual experience (Walker, 1991).

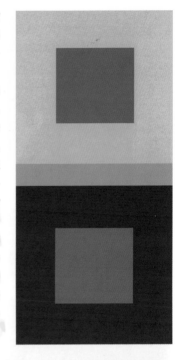

THE WATERGRAPH PROCESS

Most importantly, the children learned to apply their art knowledge to the creation of their own image and to think about the process of art as a conversation between the artist, materials and idea.

—Bruce Hucko, photographer
(Hucko, 1996, p. 3)

The greatest form of art appreciation is imitation. By exposure to various visual art periods, styles, and artists, a student will develop a greater understanding of composition, line, form, and other creative elements. A Watergraph is a watercolor rendering painted over an instant photograph, such as a Polaroid 600 Write-On picture, or a matte-finish image. Revered artist and art historian and author of *A Moveable Museum*, Gloria

Rzadko-Henry (2005) developed this unique process in her quest to find a method to help students explore art history. While sitting on the carpet of her father's photographic studio, three-year-old Rzadko-Henry painted discarded black-and-white proofs with half-used tubes of photo-oil paints. As a child, these were her coloring books. Utilizing her artistic childhood foundation, she now travels throughout the country working with thousands of educators and students who are inspired by her lectures, art exhibitions, and workshops.

By interpreting a favorite painting or style using this simple, hands-on process, her students are able to develop a much greater appreciation and understanding for art. The more she experimented with it, the more she discovered how indispensable a tool this could be for any classroom teacher. She created these Watergraphs from the inspiration of artists such as Vincent van Gogh and Berthe Morisot.

Since Rzadko-Henry's introduction of the Watergraph process in 1997, teachers throughout the country have refined and expanded on the original concept, developing new and exciting projects for their students. These teachers have encouraged their students to learn, explore, and challenge themselves through art. The Watergraph process offers students a true opportunity to appreciate art on several different levels, while allowing teachers to enhance their curriculum in a way that is both fun and successful for all students of all abilities. The process begins with visual communication in the form of a photograph. By exploring the various artists in history as well as the corresponding art periods, students begin painting on the image and take their visual language to an artistic level. This creative process allows the visual learner to encode, decode, and communicate, thereby making it unique to each student.

Materials

- Matte-finish photographs
- Watercolor pencils
- Watercolor tube paints
- Water-soluble oil pastels
- Small brushes (#1 or smaller)
- Cotton swabs/toothpicks/water/paper towels
- Fixative spray

Step 1. Inspiration. Begin by selecting an image that inspires you. Your inspiration might come from a postcard from your visit to a museum or gallery, an art history reference book, calendars, greeting cards, and so on.

Step 2. Your Canvas. Make two identical photographs with Polaroid 600 Write On film or images created on matte-finish photo paper. One photo will remain unpainted and serve as a "before" image. Reach for creative freedom, and imagine yourself in Van Gogh's studio or Monet's garden.

Step 3. Background. Paint on the second photograph's matte surface using water-soluble watercolor pastels, pencils, and liquid watercolor paints. Remember, anything that marks on paper will mark on this surface. Reproduce the exact elements, style, and colors found in the inspiration. Often tedious, this process serves as homage to a great work of art and allows you to feel like a protégé to a master. The rigidity of this activity will keep the hand and eye coordinated to emulate the original painting stroke-for-stroke.

Note that keeping the background simple will be helpful in highlighting the subject matter. Mixing the watercolor pencils with water helps to soften the pigments. Applying the wet pencil to the surface is your first opportunity to eliminate unessential details. Start with the background, blocking out unwanted objects. Avoid the heavy use of black paint by choosing instead the richness of royal blue. Try not to encourage the use of black pencils with students; Rzadko-Henry believes that the study of color and its effects is best learned and illustrated by color placement. For instance, look carefully at a shadow; notice that it is not black. Shadows are shades of the color of the object on which the shadow falls, and can be duplicated

by a mixture of complementary colors from the artist's palette. A painting will have a greater depth of field if darkened areas are a celebration of complementary colors.

Step 4. Foreground. Background colors are generally mute. Begin working in the subject with neutral-based colors. Strengthen the colors using cotton swabs and toothpicks to blend and etch the colors. To allow the likeness of facial features to bleed through, use a wet brush of diluted flesh tones very lightly to wash over the skin areas. Be aware that colors that dry on this palette can be saved and brought back by the addition of water.

Step 5. Detail. Try mixing media. Experiment with colors and strokes. No rules apply here in terms of painting the surface. This "canvas" is for you to expand on with your own interpretive style. Sharpened watercolor pencils provide the ultimate control, as do extra-fine paintbrushes. Spray the finished Watergraph with a watercolor art fixative or hairspray.

Creativity is contagious.

—Gloria Rzadko-Henry

ROLE-PLAY AND DRAMA

The number one phobia in all Americans is public speaking (Wallechinsky, Wallace, & Irving, 1977). It even shadows the fear of death and disease. How can this be true? Prevalent in the Affective Learning Style, Brain-Compatible Strategies, and Howard Gardner's Linguistic Intelligence, peer interaction, humor, drama, and role-play are ways to optimize learning. Perhaps classroom instruction does not stress the importance of drama and role-play. Perhaps we shy

away from practices that do not naturally fall into the core subject areas, which is why our system weighs assessment versus authentic assessment.

Humans' propensity to process visual information and develop a visual language is innate. We are brought into this world hard-wired with the ability to visually encode and decode. In contrast, spoken and written language must be learned. Because our comfort zone remains in the visual translation of information, these innate skills eventually begin to complement the spoken and written language as well. We translate words into images and our imaginations allow us to play movies in our mind's eye. The whole-brain learner thereby fine-tunes a perfect blend of visual processing with analytical thought. The right-brain begins working with the left-brain while constructing bridges. When the word "giraffe" is heard, most people imagine the physical animal and not the series of letters that compose the word. We think in pictures and are taught in words.

It is possible to create divergent and creative thinkers through role-play, peer interaction, and drama. Students trained at a very young age can be taught methods and techniques that will naturally enhance their ability to develop holistic thinking. If every teacher in this country taught some public-speaking technique that would apply to core subjects and creative thinking, twenty years from now public speaking would no longer be the number one phobia in America. Still, sometimes we have to search beyond the boundaries of the educational realm to find unique strategies—to embrace an all-inclusive blend of psychomotor, sensual, intellectual, imaginational, and emotional methodology.

The Meisner Technique

Sanford Meisner (1905–1997) was born and raised in New York City. Although his family expected him to go into the clothing industry, Meisner was drawn to the theatre. The basis of his technique is that the actor must be doing something "real," allowing the audience to experience real happenings—utilizing the moment to play off the other actors' behaviors. The Meisner Technique is an interdependent series of exercises that build on one another. Meisner students work on a series of progressively complex exercises that enhance the ability to improvise, to acquire an emotional life, and finally to bring the spontaneity of improvisation and the nature of personal response to text.

The most rudimentary exercise in Meisner training is called "repetition." Two actors face each other and "repeat" their observations about one another back and forth in a ping-pong fashion. An example of such an exchange might be "You're frowning." "I'm frowning." "You're frowning!" "Yes, I'm frowning." Actors are literally altering each other's behavior. Since there are no predetermined objectives, the actions are real and are part of the moment. Later, as the exercise progresses in intricacies to include "given situations," "relationships," "actions and barriers," this skill remains vital. From start to finish—from repetition to rehearsing a lead role—the components of "listening and responding" and "staying in the moment" are necessary to the work of an actor.

The Meisner Technique relies heavily on visual language. Through these exercises, students create a visual language while understanding the visual language of their partner. They then respond with words and role-play and drama begins to unfold. Regardless of the subject being taught, the Meisner Technique is easily integrated into the lesson.

A Meisner Activity for the Classroom

After a reading assignment, divide students into pairs. Choose a scene from the story. The students should then close their eyes and use the visuals from their imaginations to create a moment for themselves. Who am I? Where am I? What time is it? What am I doing? Why am I doing it? The next step is to bring the visual imagination to life and do an improvisation based on the story. Encourage the students to respond to one another's actions and expressions. There is no right or wrong in this activity; each student comes from his or her own place. The more students are taught visualization techniques, the stronger their creative-thinking skills will become. Creating an inner life through imaginative thought then bringing it to life for others through motor skills and vocabulary is a wonderful way to promote holistic thinking, while emphasizing a key component of brain-compatible strategies and the affective learning style.

MATERIAL ACQUISITION

It is no secret that many teachers are used to "low or no" budgets. The average teacher spends in excess of $500 a year out of pocket for classroom supplies. Here are some ideas to assist you in the acquisition of materials.

Fund Raising. Car wash, bake sale, candy sale, school functions, school store, and PTA/PTO.

Donations. Schoolwide material drive for parents, relatives, and neighbors. You may wish to display your students' work in the school's entrance or lobby and inform parents of its location so they can see the worthy cause their donations support. Consider asking local businesses (banks, restaurants, department stores) for donations.

Small businesses might be willing to donate materials if it means bringing customers through their doors. Propose that grocery-store managers donate materials based on a specified dollar amount of accumulated store receipts. Discussions with owners of large businesses often lead to educational support through donations. Remember, the squeaky wheel gets the grease!

Supplies. Include needed materials in the option column of your student supply lists. Some of these desired materials may be available to you through your district's central warehouse. Include materials options on your yearly "wish list."

Grants. Program proposals. Many school districts facilitate grants or minigrants from within or outside the district. These grants are usually competitive and stem from innovative, classroom-based programs. Grants usually range from $250 to $1,500.

Gifts. Teacher gifts from parents or faculty gift exchanges. It is no secret that teachers receive heartfelt gifts from students during the holidays. At the risk of sounding insensitive, you can only use so many "my favorite teacher" coffee cups or wooden apples. Find a tactful way to encourage parents to share their holiday cheer with gifts that are to be used with the students, such as film, educational videos, educational games, etc.

Photo Journalism Support. Many businesses support such organizations as Special Olympics, International Festivals, or Educational Retreats. Students using cameras to document these events may receive support from the media.

Bulk Purchasing. Buying anything in bulk or multipacks typically means lower prices. You might consider teaming with other teachers or schools for bulk material acquisition.

Visual Communication Skills for English Language Learners

5

According to the Office of English Language Acquisition, Language Enhancement, and Academic Achievement for Limited English Proficient Students (OELA), it is estimated that more than five million English language learners (ELLs) were enrolled in public primary and secondary schools for the 2003–04 school year (Padolsky, 2006). This number represents approximately 10.3 percent of total public school student enrollment, and a 43.9 percent increase over the reported 1993–94 public school ELL enrollment.

The National Teachers of English to Speakers of Other Languages (TESOL) Standards for English Language Learners PreK–12 are as follows:

> To use English to communicate in social settings: Students will use English to participate in social interactions; Students will interact in, through, and with spoken and written English for personal expression and enjoyment; Students will use learning strategies to extend their communicative competence; To use English to achieve academically in all content areas: Students will use English to interact in the classroom; Students will use English to obtain, process, construct, and provide subject matter information in spoken and written form; Students will use appropriate learning strategies to construct and apply academic knowledge; To use English in socially and culturally appropriate ways: Students will use the appropriate language variety, register, and genre according to audience, purpose, and setting; Students will use

nonverbal communication appropriate to audience, purpose, and setting; and Students will use appropriate learning strategies to extend their socio-linguistic and socio-cultural competence. (TESOL, n.d.)

Many students whose mother tongue is not English and who have difficulty learning English have difficulty learning to read in their native language, as well. Researchers at the University of California reviewed the common underlying cognitive processes to see if difficulties in one could predict difficulties in the other. Their study established that, while related, the two problems have different underlying causes (Swanson, Sáez, Gerber, & Leafstedt, 2004). Students who have difficulty learning English typically have problems with a language-independent working memory system. Students who struggle with reading are apt to have trouble with a language-specific phonological area of short-term memory. In an instructional environment, ELLs rely heavily on visual clues for the comprehension and acquisition of learning content (Olmeda, 2003).

There are many methods and materials available to assist teachers in meeting these goal-driven standards in their individual classrooms. The following visual teaching method is a unique, step-by-step approach that enables teachers to plug their students in at any given level. If the students already have the foundation set forth in the lower levels of the process, then educators can simply move their students to the next level. This method should be used to complement, not replace, existing curricula. This approach was adopted by the statewide organization "English Works in Indiana" (Gangwer and Rzadko-Henry, 2003). Authors Timothy Gangwer and Gloria Rzadko-Henry worked with the organization and developed the customized curriculum "English Works in Indiana: Tools for the Classroom" (Gangwer and Rzadko-Henry, 2003). The process moves the learner from visual communication to language acquisition by using actual photographs from the school, community, and home to create individualized journals. This individualized approach provides meaning and allows students to have ownership in the learning process. It is designed to coincide with the brain-compatible strategies outlined in previous chapters, paying particular attention to how the brain responds to different colors to increase retention.

This approach incorporates three levels:

Level 1. Visual thinking maps

Level 2. Image mapping and visual links

Level 3. Visual journals

VISUAL THINKING MAPS

Materials

Visual thinking map poster or bulletin board paper
Colored markers and pens
Instant camera and film, or digital camera and printer
Glue stick

Introduction

The goal of visual thinking maps is to allow the ELL student to create imagery that will visually communicate a central theme engaging both the kinesthetic and expressive learning modalities. Self-generated visual images powerfully simulate new ideas and insights. The immediate feedback of instant photography allows the brain to become creatively stimulated. By visually mapping these images on a poster, the student's brain will readily take on the aural, visual, and kinesthetic challenge of learning English.

Activity

Students will create ten to fifteen photographic images that represent their reflections on a chosen central theme.

Suggested Themes

Self	Home	School	Local community	Global community
Goals	Family	Academic subjects	Town/community	Cultural background
Hobbies	Lifestyle	Health and safety	Where I shop/Recreation	Native country's leaders
Friends	Activities	People at school	Civic buildings and monuments	Native country's landmarks

Steps

1. Glue the activity images to the poster with the central theme image in the center.

2. Glue the other images so they radiate from the center in order of priority.

3. Personalize each image by drawing on the poster with colored markers or pens.

4. Expand on the photograph with visual metaphors that represent key words and connections.

5. Group common images with arrows, bubbles, and lassos. (The addition of simple color, shapes, and lines radiating from the center allows the student to tap into the stored data in his or her mind.)

6. The encoding (communicating with an image) process begins here in the native "visual" tongue.

7. The key is to communicate with a personal set of symbols (see "Symbol Ideas") and experiences.

8. No artistic ability is required. The only criterion is to actively participate with current skills and to work with symbols that will easily be recognized by the student later.

9. Upon completion, these photographs become the building blocks for Level 2: Image Mapping.

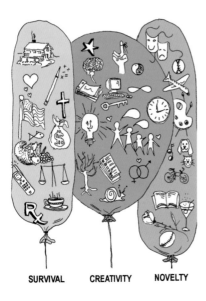

SURVIVAL   CREATIVITY   NOVELTY

Keep in mind . . .

- The mapping process requires the use of both hemispheres of the brain, which reflects the natural thinking process.
- These are visual thoughts. Use them to foster creativity and stimulate visual thinking skills.
- Maps are personal. Learning is more relevant and uniquely embedded in a meaningful context.

IMAGE MAPPING

Materials

- Image mapping cards or 8″ × 10″ paper
- Colored markers or pens
- Instant camera and film, or digital camera and printer
- Glue stick
- Investigative tools, such as magazines and the Internet

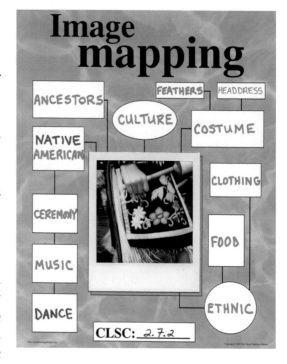

Introduction

Prewriting is written exploration before written expression is fully developed, and is based on what one knows about a subject. In this exercise, playing nonlyrical background music will stimulate one or more of the multiple intelligences and help to reinforce language acquisition through learning by association. This exercise will also help reinforce the key visual thinking skills required for this activity. Students will readily articulate from a photograph they have created because it has personal relevance.

Steps

1. Select an instant image from the Visual Mapping activity based on a chosen theme.

2. Attach the photograph to the center of the Image Mapping page.

3. Clearly print one descriptive word in the bubble above the image. Use different ink colors for parts of speech (verbs—green, nouns—red, and adjectives—blue). This increases retention.

4. Take five minutes to make written observations while looking at the selected photograph. Ask yourself, "What do I see? What do I know? How do I feel about this image?"

5. Write your responses in the outlying spaces provided.

6. Avoid complete sentences as you fill in the circles and boxes. Key words or phrases work best.

7. Allow one thought to generate another and illustrate those links by connecting words in a line.

8. Relax and let your thoughts flow. There is no right or wrong response.

Additional Activities

- At the end of the five minutes, have students trade images and assign their own thoughts and word relationships to this new photograph.
- Have students share the image (but not the theme) while asking fellow students to select the theme from a list of possibilities. Next, ask the photographer to share the theme utilizing oral practice or minimal writing skills.
- Have Student A make an image and share it with Student B. Have Student B create an image based on his or her interpretation of the image. Have Student B repeat the process with Student C. Continue this process to make a chain of related images to encourage further observational oral and written clustering exercises.

VISUAL LINKS

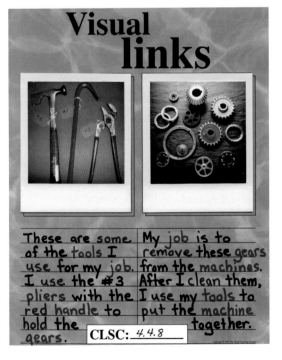

Materials

Visual links cards or 8″ × 10″ paper

Colored markers and pens

Instant camera and film, or digital camera and printer

Glue stick

Investigative tools, such as magazines and the Internet

Steps

1. Select two theme photographs from the Visual Thinking Map poster (Level 1), and the Image Mapping activity card (Level 2) to use for the Visual Links activity card.

2. Glue the two images on the Visual Links activity card.

3. Reflect on single word associations as prompts in this oral practice activity. Talk with a partner about your images and what they mean. (This intermediate activity naturally translates into a writing lesson, depending upon the ELL student's proficiency level and the interest that is generated by the selected theme.)

Key words

Anniversary -(the date
celebrating on which
marriage something
husband happened at
wife an earlier
years time)
family -(a group
friends of people
flowers connected
party by blood
beautiful or marriage)
cake cisc.7.1.3

My husband and I
are celebrating ten
years of marriage.
Our family and friends
brought this beautiful
cake to our Anniversary party.

4. Document the spoken communication by entering a brief passage or two on the lines below the photographs.

Additional Activities

- Different types of visual organization with the same images may occur as the next step in communicating the written and visual connections. As a team-building activity, have the students coordinate the images in theme categories. Encourage creativity.
- Have students generate lists of relationships that exist in their world. These should be examples of interdependency. Keep the list basic (farmers' crops to grocery store to refrigerator to cooking dinner, or oil well to gas station to car to driving to work, etc.). Have them make photographs to illustrate the lists.
- Have the students photograph and interview coworkers or fellow students. Have them use the Visual Links activity cards to document their interviews.
- Have the students make photos of various people working, then use the two image spaces on the Visual Links activity card to represent the positive and negative aspects of the job. Have them create different categories to organize jobs by pay scale, degree requirement, full or part time, physical requirements, etc.
- Have the students photograph landmarks in the community. Work with them to relate the landmarks to history, cultural significance, local or federal government, etc.
- Have the students use a series of Visual Links activity cards to document their own places of employment. Encourage the use of images and words to highlight the company's products or services.

Key words

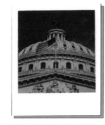

Capitol	–(the building
building	used by the
fifty	United States
thirteen	Congress for
citizen	meetings)
American	– (a citizen
vote	of the
freedom	United States)
state	
nation	
allegiance	
flag	CLSC: 5.2.4

This is the Capitol building. The American flag has fifty white stars and thirteen red and white stripes.

fire	Feuer
extinguish	Löschen Sie aus
job	Aufgabe
flame	Flamme
heat	Hitze
safety	Sicherheit
pin	Nadel
squeeze	Druck
trigger	Drücker
gear CLSC: 3.4.2	Gang

In my job there is always a chance of something catching fire. We have to know how to extinguish quickly.

Key words

machine	–(a device
fixture	built to
design	use energy
motors	to do work)
connect	–(to join;
part	to unite)
red	
job	– (a position
build	of employment)
safety	
shiny	
shop CLSC: 4.4.6	

We design and build motors in the machine shop. The shiny, red fixtures are used to connect one part to another.

- Discuss ideas of friendship. Have students pose and photograph each other. Have them record information about their physical description, biographical information, tastes, opinions, and favorite activities.

VISUAL JOURNALS

Materials

- Visual journals or 5″ × 7″ spiral notebooks
- Colored markers and pens
- Instant camera and film, or digital camera and printer
- Glue stick
- Investigative tools, such as magazines and the Internet

Introduction

This activity allows the students to express themselves with words as they record their world with images. Each journal is a medium for the personalization of each student's vocabulary. As an essential aid to daily living, a photograph paired with a handful of key words becomes the link—the building blocks to developing techniques toward effective communication.

Steps

1. Select the theme journal that corresponds to the Visual Thinking Map poster (Level 1), Image Mapping activity card (Level 2), and Visual Links activity card (Level 2).

2. Glue the image onto the page.

3. Write one or more sentences that describe the image. Decode the image (tell a story).

4. On the corresponding "Key Words" page, enter in the left column twelve English words that describe objects found in the image.

5. On the corresponding "Key Words" page, enter in the right column the translated native language word or its definition, or use the word in a sentence in the English language.

Additional Activities

- Have students do a "Key Word" list from selected images. Did each person see the same things? How were they different? Are the differences due to age, gender, or country of origin?

- Some images can be a window to the photographer's world, while others are mirrors reflecting what's inside the photographer. Have students make two images. One will serve as the window, and the other as a mirror of how the photographer feels. Encourage your students to look beyond the mirror.

Key words

Anniversary	-(the date
celebrating	on which
marriage	something
husband	happened at
wife	an earlier
years	time)
family	-(a group
friends	of people
flowers	connected
party	by blood
beautiful	or marriage)
cake CLSC: 7.1.3	

My husband and I are celebrating ten years of marriage. Our family and friends brought this beautiful cake to our Anniversary party.

- Have students photograph a place and make a list of sensory details of that place. Ask them what they might hear, see, feel, smell, or taste at the location of the photo. Have them use the list and the photo to write a description that will create that place in the reader's mind.

- Have students make photographs representing various parts of a sentence (nouns, adjectives, verbs). Put them in order and write the sentences they now represent.

Key words

church	la iglesia
steeple	la aguja
cross	la cruz
pillars	los pilares
congregation	la congregación
Sunday	El domingo
service	el servicio
Bible	La biblia
Sunday school	La escuela del domingo
Pastor	El pastor
offering	ofrecer
God CLSC: 2.7.4	El dios

My family and I go to this church in our community. It is located at Walton and Church Streets.

6 Subject-Specific Visual Learning Activities for the Classroom

The following activities are subject specific, designed for the PreK to lifelong learner. Understanding the innovative talent of teachers, the activities are designed to be modified easily up or down to adjust to the appropriate grade level being taught. Keep in mind that imagery is key to all activities. Even when the activity calls for a "photograph," magazine images, hand-drawn images, animation, video stills, or existing photographs can be used. Photographs can be from 35-mm, instant, disposable, or digital cameras, as well as camera cell phones, embedded computer cameras, downloadable TV stills, YouTube stills, and Google Earth satellite images. Remember, the product of the activity is not as important as what is gained in *doing* the activity.

The following directions are addressed to the teacher unless they are in quotation marks. In that case, they are addressed to the student.

LANGUAGE ARTS

Activity 1. The Eye of the Beholder

Have students create images of things that they feel are special or beautiful. Have them describe orally or in writing why they feel the way they do. Post the images in your classroom. Ask students to photograph things that they think are beautiful that others may dismiss or think uninteresting. Have them defend their images as if in a courtroom. Have students make images of things they think are ugly in a way that emphasizes some beauty. Have them trade photographs and write about what they find beautiful in another student's way of seeing something.

Activity 2. Photo Abstractions

Create file cards with abstract concepts such as freedom, love, sacrifice, hate, joy, sorrow, independence, responsibility, honor, friendship, value, jealousy, democracy, and respect. Have students select cards at random and make photographs to represent the concept they selected. Display images on a bulletin board and have students infer the abstract from the evidence in the photographs. Students should explain their images orally or in writing. As you build a collection of concepts illustrated visually, post them together and compare what students mean when they use concepts. Post the cards on the board and have students rank concepts according to their importance to each student.

Activity 3. Photo Interpretation

Allow students to make images to interpret songs, poems, or stories. Students may choose their own piece to interpret, or ask the entire class to interpret the same piece for comparison and discussion. They can take photographs from the point of view of character or persona. Images can represent events or objects that occur in the stories. They can also depict new or different endings or twists to existing stories, poems, or songs. Reverse the process by asking learners to find music or stories that fit existing images. Ask them to make a new book or musical recording covers for songs or stories they like. Discuss how photography interprets or communicates the style, message, or theme of the work.

Activity 4. Visual Metaphors

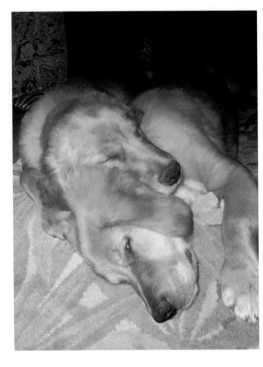

Ask students to make images (without other people in them) that are visual metaphors for their personalities. A visual metaphor can reflect values, self-concept, interests, goals, opinions, and so on. Have students create three visual metaphors for who or what they used to be, who or what they are now, or who or what they hope to be. Discuss these visual metaphor photographs in class. "Do others see you in the way you see yourself?"

Activity 5. Point of View

Ask students to imagine themselves as nonhuman subjects or objects. This might include plants, animals, or natural or manufactured objects. Have them list the things that might be important to them in their new imagined role. Who or what would they interact with on a regular basis? After discussing their lists, ask students to make images from the point of view they have chosen to imagine. When they have made their photographs, use them as a basis for stories, plays, or presentations. This activity is a good way to help students visualize and learn processes. In a science lesson, you might assign different students different roles as objects and ask them to imagine their reactions to gravity, heat, acceleration, or other physical forces. This activity is also good for building emphatic skills.

Activity 6. Phonetography

Assign students letters of the alphabet. Ask each student to find and photograph something that starts with the same initial consonant or vowel sound (A—acorn, B—book, C—cow, and so on.). Post images with letters in a visual alphabet. Highlight tough letters like Q and X. "Form words using phonetic photos."

Activity 7. See What You Mean

Have students make photographs representing various parts of a sentence (nouns, verbs, adjectives). "Put them in order and compose the sentences they now represent. Rearrange them to create different sentences." (Remember, nonsense sentences can be fun, too!) Have students assemble their own images into sentences and see if other students can read them. After photo sentences are arranged, rearrange them or leave parts out to see if they still make sense.

Activity 8. Say What You Mean

Discuss homonyms. Have students work in teams to create pairs of photographs that show words that sound alike but that do not have the same meaning. Write sentences or short stories based on the homonyms students have photographed. Challenge them to see how many pairs they can incorporate into their stories. Have students write or tell a joke based on misunderstanding a homonym. Have them repeat this activity using synonyms or antonyms. Create a class visual dictionary of homonyms, synonyms, and antonyms.

Activity 9. Local Definitions

Identify concepts, phenomena, principles, or definitions from current lessons. Assign students to make photographs to replace textbook images with local examples from their environment. Compare images and discuss student understanding of these concepts. "Look for subtle or blatant differences in comprehension. Remember, differences are not necessarily wrong; subtle differences can lead to new understanding."

Activity 10. Photo Poems

"Make an image that is dominated by a single color, then use the image to generate a list of other things that are the same color. Incorporate descriptive words and emotions inspired by the color. Produce a poem or short prose piece using the photograph as an illustration."

Activity 11. Photo Stories

Use existing photos or ask students to make new images of things that interest them. Begin by having students write literal descriptions of their photographs. "Be as specific as possible." Then expand on this by having them do one of the following:

- "Tell the story that led to the making of this photograph. What chain of events led to the creation of this image?"
- "Tell the story that begins with the taking of the photograph. Where could it go from there?"
- "If your image contains a person, make a list of real and imagined characteristics for that person (kind, weak, strong, funny). Now write a short scene describing your character's reaction to an every-day occurrence."

Activity 12. Photo Journalists

"Create a classroom newspaper including photographic stories, poems, coverage of special events, interviews, and book reviews." Photocopy the final product to distribute to students and parents.

Activity 13. Budding Authors

Students can make photographic books with text generated by images they have taken or with images used to illustrate text they have already written. Students may also want to use photos on the covers for the books or stories they have written.

Activity 14. First Impressions

"Pretend to be a creature from another planet. You have just landed on earth. Make a photographic report to send home. Write a description that will explain the images to your fellow beings on your home planet."

Activity 15. Alphabet Hunt

Have students make photographs of classroom scenes, then have them mount images on paper or cardboard and begin to list things in the

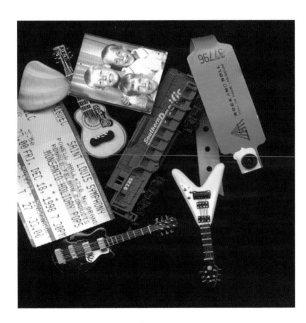

photos that start with the same letter. Have students name the objects in each photo, and determine how many objects start with each letter (for example, there are four "B" words and five "P" words in this photograph).

Activity 16. Make a Vowel Train

Create a bulletin board with a train made of construction paper. For each of the train cars, create small envelopes with vowel sounds written on them. "Take photographs of objects that are pronounced with the vowel sounds." Have students place the cards in the corresponding train car.

Activity 17. Photo Sentences

Have students organize existing photographs or newly created images into sets that create sentences. "From each photograph, make a list of nouns, verbs, and adjectives, then extend the list to include prepositional phrases and questions." Combine all of the images and sentences into individual, group, or class stories.

Activity 18. Photo Haikus

Japanese haiku poetry is based on three lines with five syllables on the first line, seven on the second line, and five on the third. Have students select and photograph scenes they like and write haikus based on their images.

Activity 19. What Comes Next?

"Photograph various everyday situations. Put all of your images into a hat." Have teams of students pick random photographs from the hat and shoot additional photographs, showing what might come next. Discuss situations and possible outcomes (banana peel on the sidewalk, someone leaning back on two chair legs, soccer goalie asleep in the goal, and so on). This also makes for a great writing lesson.

Activity 20. Storyboarding

Have students write scenes to be filmed as a movie. Have them decide on the angles for camera shots by using empty cameras, or even paper tubes (such as toilet paper or paper towel tubes). Have them do rough sketches for each camera shot (stick figures will suffice). Now have the students create photos for their storyboards based on their sketches. Have them mount their photographs on cardboard and describe each scene in writing. They can include dialogue for that scene if appropriate.

Activity 21. Prepositions

Make a list of prepositions (on top of, inside, underneath, before, and so on). Make images of students demonstrating the visual meaning of those prepositions. Post these on a bulletin board. Have each student act out or demonstrate a different preposition. Pair students with their prepositional opposite (over/under, in front of/in back of, and so on).

Activity 22. Photo Interviews

Photograph people who work in the school. Describe the person in the image. What does that person look like? What does that person do? Can we tell anything about where the person works based on the photo? "Interview those people, using these starter questions: What do you like or dislike about the work? What type of special knowledge do you need to do this job effectively? Write a report to accompany the image."

Activity 23. Out-of-the-Box Stories

"Brainstorm a list of characters, objects, and places. Photograph the story elements and place the images in different boxes, each representing characters, objects, or places. Pick three photos, one from each box, and write a story using the images as inspiration. Trade one of the three photographs with a classmate and see how it changes the original story."

Activity 24. Comparisons

"Select a set of simple, comparative, and superlative words (far–farther–farthest) and make a single image that illustrates all three adjectives. Try making three separate photos for the selected adjectives. Swap images and write sets of descriptive sentences using simple, comparative, and superlative words. Some adjectives are difficult to photograph. Discuss why some are more difficult than others."

Activity 25. Photo Riddles

"Make images from the point of view of nonsentient objects, then write a riddle with three sentences that could help you guess the object. Remember to photograph from the point of view of the object. Do not photograph the object itself." Example: "Hands grab me all day long. They turn and twist me. Sometimes I let you in and sometimes I lock you out. What am I?" "A doorknob!"

Activity 26. Tall Tales

"Make a list of exaggerations. Discuss how to make these exaggerations come to life with photography. Make an image that exaggerates some person or thing. Try shooting from low angles. Shoot from above. Photograph a person in the foreground who dominates some larger background object. Create a 'tall tale' that uses the image as a major element of the narrative."

Activity 27. Photo Comics

"Script a story and photograph it. Mount the photographs on a layout board. Add dialogue balloons. Self-sticking labels can be cut into the shape of balloons and stuck directly onto the image." Photography stores and craft stores generally sell these dialogue balloons.

Activity 28. Advertisements

Discuss visual appeal in advertising. Ask the students, "What role does photography play in advertising?" Have them give examples of how it is used. Look at actual examples of photographic advertisements with them. Have students write and photograph advertisements for the school, a novel, the community, a sports event, or a favorite object. Display advertisements and discuss their effectiveness.

Activity 29. Autobiography

Have students make self-portraits or portraits of each other. Have them gather images of themselves at younger ages. Use the photographs to outline an autobiography. "Describe who you were in each image and how you have changed from photo to photo." As an alternative, have students use other students' photos to interview them and write biographies of one another.

Activity 30. Metaphorically Seeing

Discuss human qualities and personality traits. "Pick a person and make a list of that person's personality traits and qualities. Concentrate on a few of the most distinctive traits, then photograph an object that shares those traits. Working with the images and the list, write a description of the person using the photograph as a central metaphor ('My dad is an oak tree because . . .')." Discuss how similes are different from metaphors. "Make a photo metaphor of yourself."

Activity 31. Main Ideas

"Locate or create images that clearly communicate main ideas. Write the main idea at the top of a sheet of paper. List all of the supporting details in the photograph that contribute to the main idea." Ask them to write a unified paragraph that communicates and supports the main idea using the image and the notes. "Try using three photos to help write a three-paragraph essay."

Activity 32. Word Pictures

"Photograph a place and make a list of sensory details of that place. What might you hear, see, feel, smell, or taste at the location of this image? Use the list and the photo to write a description that will create that place in a reader's mind."

Activity 33. Context

"In groups, choose an object small enough to be portable, but large enough to photograph well. Think up as many outlandish contexts for the object as possible (a desk in the woods, a lamp at a picnic, and so on).

Decide on the most unusual setting and make a photograph of the object in that setting. Discuss how the new context affects our understanding of the object. How would other settings change our understanding? Write a short story that details a fictional account of how the object came to be in the context of the image."

Activity 34. Stream of Consciousness

"Discuss ways to make unintentional photographs.
1. Close your eyes, spin around, point, and shoot.
2. Take an image from your chest, waist, or knee level.
3. Shoot to music.
4. Shoot while you are walking or running.
"Create an unintentional photograph. Write down everything that comes to mind from the image. Using your notes and the image, write a stream-of-consciousness monologue."

Activity 35. Stereotypes

"Discuss and make a list of some common stereotypes. Draft some interview questions for each stereotype and predict the answers. Photograph people who seem to fit the stereotype. Interview those people with the prepared questions. Compare the subject's answers with your predicted answers. Display the photographs and try to match the questions and answers to the correct images. Create and write about a fictional character based on the stereotype images."

Activity 36. Character Sketch

"List the characters in a literary work. Find and photograph people who look like characters in literature. Did you make the selection based on physical description or some other criterion? Using the image, develop a character sketch describing why the person in the photograph looks like the character. Relate details in image to details in the literary work. Write a mock interview with the character."

Activity 37. Book Covers

Discuss the relationship between book covers and the stories inside the book. Is there a thematic relationship? How does a book cover symbolize its theme? Discuss some symbols that occur in literature being studied in class. "Make images and incorporate them into new book cover designs.

Use characters, setting, plot, and theme as symbolic elements of the cover. Try making a photographic book cover for the story of your life."

Activity 38. Fact and Opinion

Discuss the difference between fact and opinion. Select one photograph and pass it around the class. "Tell one thing that you can tell for certain because it is evident in the image." (Each student has to reveal something new.) Ask students to begin making inferences based on the same photo. "Try writing an editorial for a newspaper that conveys an opinion based on the facts and the photograph."

Activity 39. Conflict and Dialogue

Discuss situations that produce conflict (bicycles and cars, young and old generations, two children and one toy, and so on). "Make photographs illustrating types of conflicts. Use them to write a dialogue between the objects of conflict. What would they say to each other? How might the conflict be resolved? Create a photo comic strip of conflict resolutions."

Activity 40. Cause and Effect

Discuss possible subjects for before-and-after advertisements. "Look at magazine advertisements that imply cause-and-effect relationships. Create before-and-after advertisement images. Identify the implied cause of change and the implied effect."

Activity 41. Reading Cards

Have students choose things whose names they want to learn to read. "Photograph one thing and mount it on cardboard. Write the name of that object on the card." If the name is written on the back of the card, it can be used as a flashcard. If it is on the front of the card, it can form a visual dictionary for new vocabulary words.

Activity 42. Action Words

Discuss and list common classroom activities that can be photographed. Have students photograph one another while engaged in such activities. Use the images to stimulate language development. Ask questions about the images. Have students write or dictate sentences about each photograph.

Activity 43. Image Clustering

"Make or select an image and attach it to the center of a large sheet of paper. Take the next five minutes to make quick notes about the associations that come to mind when looking at the photograph. Use boxes or circles to highlight a specific idea. Link the ideas to the image with a line. If the idea makes you think of another idea, link the two ideas with a line. Use key words and phrases. Do not worry about spelling and punctuation. Use this activity to help discover what you know or think you know about any subject. Use your image cluster notes to begin more formal writing."

Activity 44. Thinking With Images

Have the class select a photographic subject. Have one student photograph that subject and show it to the next student. That student then makes an image based on what the photograph of the previous student suggests to him or her. This should not be a copy, but a point of departure. Use the images for group clustering activities.

Activity 45. Story Starters

In many stories, doors, windows, and openings mark the beginning of wonderful adventures. Have students make images of doors, windows, and openings. Give them a set amount of time to brainstorm as many possible explanations of what may lie on the other side of the opening. Nothing is too wild—if they can imagine it, they should write it. Have them save their story-starter ideas for future creative writing assignments.

Activity 46. Writing Visually

Have students begin by making images of scenes they find interesting. "Write a paragraph describing your photo in detail." At the conclusion of a preset amount of time, have students put all photos into a hat; have students select the photos at random. "Read the description on the photo you picked. When you are certain that the description matches the photograph you are holding, stand up." There could be points awarded for accurate correct matches and penalties for standing for the wrong description.

Activity 47. Living Viewfinders

Have students observe things through camera viewfinders and make written notes of what they see. The presence of some type of viewfinder to restrict vision helps clarify and focus observational skills. Have students imagine themselves as both still and motion picture viewfinders. How would their descriptive notes differ? "Practice writing the action as well as describing the scene."

Activity 48. Making Visual Connections

Have students form teams of five or more. Assign or have them select a theme from which to make photographs. Each student should create one image on the assigned or selected theme. Students may plan and organize their image making, or work independently. After making their images, students should attach all the photographs to a board in a way that makes some sense visually. Each student should then write a brief paragraph linking the image to the one next to it. Discuss forms of visual organization (spatial, chronological, thematic, narrative, geographical, and so on). "Can you find examples of writing that is organized on similar principles?"

Activity 49. Smooth Moves

Have students photograph each other acting out emotions or adopting attitudes. Make a list of emotions and assign as necessary to ensure a large-enough variety of images from which to choose. Have students select and photograph a variety of different objects. Place the object and the emotion photos on a table and allow students to take turns selecting images to post on a bulletin board. Each new image must further the narrative that has been started. Discuss the telling of stories as the linking of strong visual images. Have students discuss how this might help them with their own storytelling.

Activity 50. Mirrors and Windows

Some photos can be regarded as windows of the world. They show us a view of the world and provide glimpses of things we may not see on our own. Other images are more like mirrors. They reflect the photographer and reveal inner thoughts. Have students make two images: one representing a window, the other illustrating the mirror. Encourage students to write about their photographs.

Activity 51. A Picture Is Worth a Thousand Words

Have students photograph a problem or concern they have (racial tension, pollution, condition of the school, and so on). Then have them use the image to compose a letter to persuade someone to help change the situation. Remind them to

1. introduce themselves and explain why they care about this issue;

2. state the problem clearly, but avoid attaching blame;

3. offer assistance or a variety of solutions;

4. write as though the person they are addressing wants to solve the problem as much as they do; and

5. close with a specific call for action.

Activity 52. Visual Problem Solving

It often helps to define clearly a problem before attempting to solve it. This is called *analytical writing*. Images can help focus analytical writing. Have students photograph things they see as problems. Ask them to write about their images using the following steps:

1. Identify the problem (not the cause or solution).

2. Identify who might find this to be a problem. Is it just one person or is it a group of people with common concerns?

3. Brainstorm a list of at least five possible causes of the problem. If there are explanations for the causes, link them in a chain. Remember, most problems are complex or they would have been solved already. Use the photograph to stay on track. After you have completed all of the steps, begin to list possible solutions.

Activity 53. Magical Adventures

This activity was originally designed for senior citizens. They made four images of people, animals, or objects that were important to them. The images were provided to student writing teams. The teams were asked to make up names for each character in the images, choose magical objects from the photos, and weave them together into magical adventure stories. The stories were then read to the senior citizens. This could easily be adapted by students in different grades instead of senior citizens.

Activity 54. My Body Is a Metaphoto

Have students make photographs that are metaphors for their physical bodies. "Use the images to write short stories that begin with the sentence 'My body is . . . '"

Activity 55. Book Review Photo Cubes

Have students make images based on a book they have read by becoming a character and photographing a reenactment of an event in the story or making images without people that tell about the story. "Assemble construction paper cubes and attach photos and writings about the book being reviewed (as well as the title) on each side of the cube." One cube becomes the book review for each book. Keep the cubes on display and allow students to use them to decide which books they want to read.

Activity 56. Directions

Have students photograph scenes that interest them, then have them write detailed instructions for another student to duplicate that same photo. Without showing the original photos to each other, have students exchange written descriptions and create photos based on those descriptions. Compare the results. Discuss why the images look similar or different.

Activity 57. Photo Messages

Have students imagine messages they might want to convey to other students in class. Have them write those messages and make images that specifically communicate their messages. Have students exchange photos and record the messages they perceive from the photos. "Compare them to the intended message. Are some forms of information easier to communicate than others? List the types of information photography best communicates. List the types of information words best communicate."

Activity 58. A Day in My Life

Have students make photographs that represent a day in their lives. This can be a long-term project where students check out a class camera to photograph at home. It may take several months for all the students to complete this project. After they have the images, mount them in a journal or on a poster and have students write about their days.

Activity 59. Motivator Graphs

Select a number of books you would like students to read during the semester. Create a bar graph with the book covers or titles as one row of information. Make images of each student in the class and photocopy enough of them for the number of books you have selected. As students read the books, they can place the trimmed photocopy of their image in the appropriate column of the bar graph. This tells you which books are being read the most and who is doing the reading.

Activity 60. What a Day for a Daydream

Have students make photos inspired by a recent dream or daydream. "Write or verbalize a short explanation about why you chose to make this particular image. What things in a photograph can suggest that it is a dream image? Expand this by keeping a dream or daydream journal."

Activity 61. Sounds Like . . .

"Make images of things that make sounds." Use them as flashcards by asking students to make the sound they see in the photograph. "Listen to a piece of music and make a photograph of how that music makes you feel. Expand on this by making images of things with specific smells and tastes." Discuss the words we use to describe sounds, smells, and tastes.

Activity 62. Vocabulary Scavenger Hunt

Organize a scavenger hunt to find and photograph a list of vocabulary words. Students often take particular pride in learning to spell and pronounce the vocabulary words they photograph.

Activity 63. Author Shots

When attending state or national conferences, take your camera to photograph authors in attendance. Have them sign the photograph and post them on the bulletin board back at school. Help students feel connected to the authors of the books they are reading. As an extension, have students pose for photos as authors of their own books.

Activity 64. Figuratively Speaking

Make a list of figurative expressions (time flies, throwing in the towel, heard it from the grapevine, and so on). Assign teams of students to make images depicting these figurative expressions. Post them on a bulletin board and discuss them. Where did those expressions originate?

Activity 65. Fact and Fiction

Have students photograph and interview other students. Each student should write one piece about the student that is factual and based on the interview, and one piece that is fictional and based on imagination. Combine the writing and photograph on a poster or in a book.

Activity 66. Photo Diary Twist

Prepare a master diary page with three-hole-punch paper. Include a dotted two- to three-inch circle on the master page. Copy and distribute the pages on a regular basis, asking students to cut out the circles on their pages and then record important recent events. A photo of the student is attached to the inside back cover so that the face shows through the cutout circle of every page. No matter how many pages are added, every page will include the student's image.

Activity 67. Computer Stories

Photographs can be scanned into computers, or digital images can be placed on pages with layout programs. This is a nice way to get the student thinking about the links between the written word and the electronic image. It also allows for seamless integration of images and text.

Activity 68. Photo Myths

Discuss mythology and the elements found in myths of various cultures. List these elements. Use photographs of students in the class as the basis for creating and writing myths. Make sure everyone becomes a mythological character with special powers.

MATH

Activity 69. Math Concept Search

Discuss mathematical concepts, ideas, or processes. Divide students into teams and ask them to find and photograph examples of those concepts in the world around them. Ask them to photograph things that require an understanding of mathematical or geometrical concepts to work or to have been created. Follow this with writing assignments to explore further the connections between mathematics and the world.

Activity 70. Math Manipulatives

Assign the numerals 0 to 10 to different student teams. Have those teams find or assemble objects to photograph as representations of those numerals (two pencils, four cards, six books, and so on). Duplication adds variety once the basic numbers are all photographed. Attach these photographs to cards to use as manipulatives. By creating and photographing signs for addition, subtraction, multiplication, and division, students can create math problems for each other as a simple math game (2 pencils + 7 marbles × 4 cards = ?).

Activity 71. Coordinate Geometry

Photograph an empty wall or large bulletin board from a marked spot on the floor in front of it. Lay a sheet of transparent material over the image and draw a grid system over it. Assign numbers and directions or numbers and letters to the grid to plot coordinates. Have teams place cards with numerals or photographs of fellow students on the wall or bulletin board. Have them rephotograph the wall and use the transparency to plot the location of one of the items they have placed on the wall. Have students or student teams use the grid overlay and the original photograph to try to select the correct item based on the coordinate information. Photograph sites around the school from overhead views and repeat the above process to locate objects. Discuss maps, navigation, and surveying.

Activity 72. Creating by the Numbers

Some art forms use numerical patterns or mathematical formulae to generate them. Show some examples from an art history textbook (or ask for help from your art teacher or art resource person). Look for examples by artists such as Mondrian, Albers, Vasarely, and Noland. Ask students to find and photograph art forms that rely on principles that can be expressed mathematically or geometrically. Computer screens reduce images to mathematical formulae; even color reproduction in magazines is based on the number of dots of a specific color per square inch.

Activity 73. Divide and Conquer

Photograph an object that is made up of many parts. Count how many parts make up the "whole" in the image. Discuss the purpose of counting the number of parts that make up a whole. Hide portions of the photograph to show fractions. Discuss how knowing the idea of one part of a whole made up of equal parts can lead you to the area of the whole.

Activity 74. Form Finders

Divide students into teams. Assign each team a 3-D form such as a cube, sphere, cylinder, or pyramid. Have each team member photograph an example of his or her assigned shape then attach images to large sheets of paper. Send students back to measure the shapes they photographed. Record measurements on paper. Have each student write his or her name on the paper, carefully remove the photograph, and attach it to a fresh sheet of paper. Students then trade photos with other students and measure the new shapes. To determine if they have done accurate measurements, compare the results with the original measurements. Have students determine volumes based on their measurements.

Activity 75. Groups and Sets

Make images of different groupings of things in twos, threes, and fours. Use these photographs to teach that the recognition of groups can lead to the quick solution of problems. Introduce the concepts of "greater than" and "less than" by pairing photos.

Activity 76. Manipulative Organizers

Use photographs as markers for storage containers for manipulatives. Also consider photographing manipulatives and using them to designate the student responsible for those manipulatives that week. This can help build responsibility in students for their own learning.

Activity 77. Math Business Games

Visit a bank and document it with photographs. (Be sure to secure permission from management prior to making images.) Use the images as markers in the classroom. Divide students into teams of five or six and have them form their own banks. Ask them to create a logo and advertising slogan for the bank. Do group photographs to build team spirit. Create your own classroom currency and distribute some to each student. The students must deposit their money in a bank other than the bank where they work. Set up checking accounts for every student and set aside banking hours for transaction. Everyone should have a chance to be a teller to practice adding and subtracting. Allow students to use classroom money to buy privileges. Encourage students to check the math on their deposits and withdrawals. Try setting up class businesses. Introduce percentages by discussing interest for savings or loans.

Activity 78. Math in the Marketplace

Have students photograph their favorite products and brainstorm on the math concepts or skills that were required to produce those products. Have students photograph their favorite sports or entertainment activity and discuss the requisite math skills for those activities (statistics for evaluating and improving performance, accounting for keeping track of money, probability for predicting events, and so on).

Activity 79. Math Scavenger Hunts

Send student teams with cameras to find and photograph mathematical concepts from a teacher-generated list: a prime number, an equilateral triangle, an even number divisible by eight, and so on.

Activity 80. Number Codes

Ask students to write out the alphabet and assign numbers to each letter (A—1, B—2, C—3, and so on). This becomes their code sheet. Have them photograph different scenes or objects around the classroom. Using their code sheets, they should then write one or two sentences describing their image. Post all of the photos on the bulletin board. Have students choose images other than their own to decipher what the descriptions read.

Activity 81. Photo Geometry

Photograph objects that have slopes or angles. Draw a grid onto the photograph with a permanent marker. Allow students to calculate the slope of various real-life objects such as windshields, rooflines, or bicycle handlebars.

Activity 82. Photo Enlargements With Coordinate Geometry

Have students photograph a single shape or object they would like to enlarge. Lay tracing paper or transparency material over the image and draw a grid pattern on it with quarter-inch or half-inch squares. On a sheet of drawing paper, draw a light pencil grid with the same number of lines and squares, but make the squares two or three inches in size. Plot key drawing points on the small grid and transfer them to the larger grid. Draw lightly at first and darken lines after the image is complete. Older students can be challenged with more-complex images to draw from or by expanding to larger sizes. Try assigning each learner one square of the grid to draw on a large square of paper. Reassemble the squares and compare them to the original photograph.

Activity 83. Photo Fractions

Have students make photographs of fractions and even decimals to use as manipulatives. Encourage them to find subjects that are easily divided or already divided into equal parts. Post the photo fractions or use them as flashcards.

Activity 84. Photo Graphs

Make images of each student in class. Create a generic bar graph on the bulletin boards with columns the same width as the photographs. At the end of each day, remove the previous day's photographs and store them in a box. Post a new subject or question for the bar graph. Questions or columns might begin with simple divisions of boys and girls, ages, hair color, and so on. Expand the columns to do opinion surveys such as the favorite flavor of ice cream in the class. Transform the picture graphs to other representational graphs such as circular or linear. Discuss why graphs communicate information more clearly. Ask students if they could devise a graph that was both correct and misleading. Discuss making inferences from the graphs.

Activity 85. Photo Lines

Photograph examples of lines. Lay tracing paper over the images and trace the lines. What type of lines are they (straight, curved, wavy, sharp, crooked, jagged, broken)? If this line had its own personality, what would it be like? What might it say?

Activity 86. Photo Poems by the Numbers

Some art forms rely on a numbered formula to create variety within a disciplined set of rules. Japanese haiku poetry is based on three lines with five syllables on the first line, seven syllables on the second line, and five on the third. Have students select and photograph scenes they like, then compose haikus based on their images.

Activity 87. Photo Set Diagrams

Have students make full-body images of each other. Using circles of string as boundaries, arrange the photographs in Venn diagram form to illustrate the concepts of intersecting sets, nonintersecting sets, and subsets. Use photographs from other lessons to create different set categories.

Activity 88. Math Photo Storyboarding

Have students create photo storyboards of the steps necessary to solve various mathematical problems. Discuss and justify the steps included in the storyboard. Display the steps on the bulletin board.

Activity 89. Ratio and Proportion

Have students photograph each other in standing poses. "Calculate the ratio of arm length to body length on the person's actual body. Calculate the ratio of arm length to body length in the photograph. Are the ratios the same? Why? Calculate the ratio of the size of the person in the image with the person's actual size. Use a photograph to calculate the size of a building or tree."

Activity 90. Shape Tracing

"Lay tracing paper or clear plastic acetate over photographs and trace shapes you find in images. Identify and label the shapes. Repeat this process looking for a different shape each time. Number the image and the shape tracings." After drawing the photo, students have three minutes to identify all the shapes they can see in the photo. Compare this to the shape tracings. Were all the shapes identified?

Math

Activity 91. Stopping Time

Photograph a clock and place it in the center of the bulletin board. Begin to collect and make images that represent events that take place at certain times of day. Post these images around the clock photo and link the activity depicted in the images with the corresponding time on the clock.

Activity 92. Visual Story Problems

Recycle old classroom photographs or ask students to create new images that contain critical information needed to solve a story problem. Have students write story problems to go with their images and exchange them. Remember, some important piece of information must come from the photograph itself. If Bob leaves for practice immediately, it will take him thirty minutes to get there. He has to stop and pick up his uniform at home, which will add another fifteen minutes to his trip. He can take a shortcut that will cut seven minutes off his trip. If he does all of the above, what time will he arrive at practice?

Activity 93. Visualizing Probabilities

Photograph each student in the class. Photocopy and attach each to identically shaped and sized cardboard markers. Use the markers to select students for classroom activities. Always discuss probabilities before selecting a marker from a box. With no other qualifier, what is the probability of any one student being drawn? Give students the opportunity to devise a single qualifier for a drawing that would increase the odds that they will be chosen; for instance, you must first discard any student drawn who is not wearing athletic shoes today. How much would this qualifier increase the probability of him or her being selected? Why? Now attach student images

to a cube to create photo dice, or arrange photos in a circle with a spinner in the middle. How does this arrangement change the probability of one student being selected?

Activity 94. Shape Finders

Divide students into teams. Assign each team a shape such as a circle, square, rectangle, or triangle. Have each team member photograph an example of his or her assigned shape. Attach photos to large sheets of paper. Send students back to measure the shapes they photographed. Record measurements on paper and have each student put his or her name on the paper. Carefully remove the images and attach them to fresh sheets of paper. Have students exchange photos and measure their new shapes.

Activity 95. Math Careers

Have students begin by making images that represent the careers they want for themselves. Have them use the photographs to write about the specific math skills someone in that profession might need. As a class, categorize the professions into high, medium, or low math skill professions. Make additional images to fill in the categories. Discuss the differences.

Activity 96. Solving for Height #1

Have students measure each other's height. Next, photograph a student standing by an object of unknown height. "Guess the measurement of the object if the student's height is known. Measure the height of the student and the object in the photograph and compare."

Activity 97. Solving for Height #2

Make an image from ground level of a student whose head top is directly in line with the top of a background object of unknown height. "Measure the distance from the photographer or camera to the base of the object. Measure the distance from the photographer or camera to the student being photographed. Compare your results."

Activity 98. Growth Charts

Using long strips of adding machine tape, have students measure each other by cutting the strips to their exact height. Encourage each student to decorate his or her strip. Photograph each student and attach it to the top of his or her strip. Mount these in the hall outside of the classroom. Encourage students to check their height periodically to see if they have grown.

SCIENCE

Activity 99. Categories

As a class, discuss different categories that pertain to what you are currently studying. For earth science, this might include organic and inorganic, living and dead, plant types, or animal classification. Prepare a stack of cards with categories written on them. "Photograph something that fits into the category on the card. Create a chart with categories on the bulletin board. Place photos on the chart according to the category." Discuss how categories help us to begin to understand problems better.

Activity 100. Living and Nonliving Things

Discuss the distinction between living and nonliving things. Make photographs and classify the things in the pictures that are living, nonliving, or that were once alive. Develop a scheme to classify the images. Make a special display board for photographs about which there is some disagreement among the students.

Activity 101. Watering a Wilted Plant

"Select a large, badly wilted plant. Predict the process of recovery once it is watered. How long do you think it will take the plant to recover? Will the leaves recover at the same time? Water the plant, and then photograph it. Include in the image a card showing the time the plant was watered. Make a new photo every half hour until the plant is fully recovered. Compare the photographic record with the original prediction."

Activity 102. Shadows

Discuss the relationship of light to shadow. "Find a good shadow-casting object (fire hydrant, tree, flag pole, person). Make photographs of your shadow-casting object at regular intervals throughout the course of the day. Record the time on each image. Sequence the photos and analyze the results. Measure shadow lengths. Predict shadow lengths for times of day not photographed."

Activity 103. Local Definitions

Identify concepts (phenomena, principles, or definitions) from current lessons. Assign students to make images to replace textbook photographs with local examples from their environment. Compare photographs and discuss student understanding of the concepts. Look for subtle or blatant differences in comprehension. Remember, different understandings are not necessarily wrong. Subtle differences can lead to new understanding.

Activity 104. Changing Times

Create a bulletin board or display area for documenting processes of change. Assign students to teams to design experiments that illustrate change that occurs on different time scales. Students should make every effort to document the change with photographs and annotations. "Control or record the variables in your experiment." Some examples might include a rocket launch that exchanges energy for forward motion very quickly, water (frozen) that slowly melts to water (liquid), liquid water that even more slowly changes to water (gas, or evaporated water), a plant that grows very slowly, or erosion that occurs at a much slower pace. Have students classify and compare changes by the time they take. Create a chart to compare relative life spans.

Activity 105. Visual Process Charts

Identify activities students need to perform in order to conduct experiments. Have students storyboard or script the steps necessary to perform an activity (prepare a microscope slide, prepare a culture, light a burner, clean a piece of equipment, and so on). Photograph the steps and display them on posters around the room for easy reference.

Activity 106. Equipment Organizers

Use photographs as markers for storage containers for science equipment and supplies. Also consider photographing equipment and using photos to designate the student responsible for the equipment that week. This can help build responsibility in students for their own learning.

Activity 107. Lab Notebook Imagery

Include images in lab notebooks to record progress in experiments and research. "Use photos in field notebooks to record plants and animals in a way that does not disturb the environment. Label parts of photographs and identify them in your notebook. Include measurements or something in a photograph to show scale (ruler, yardstick, person, and so on). Use glue sticks to attach photos to pages or photo-corners for easy removal."

Activity 108. Science in the Marketplace

Have students photograph their favorite products and brainstorm on the concept or skills that were required to produce those products. Have them photograph their favorite sports or entertainment activities and discuss how advances in science have affected those activities.

Activity 109. Science Scavenger Hunts

Send student teams with cameras to find and photograph things such as a machine that exchanges energy, such as a refrigerator equipped with an icemaker, an example of gravity, an example of a symbiotic relationship, a chemical change, and so on.

Activity 110. Image Collection Catalogs

Create a list of subjects that need to be photographed to create a catalog (this might include plants and animals for a catalog of local biodiversity or potential pollutants for a catalog of environmental hazards). Assemble these photographs into notebooks to have available in class. Update them frequently.

Activity 111. Photo Brainstorming

When beginning a new area of study, ask students to each make one image that represents that subject to them. "Paste the photograph onto a large sheet of paper and begin to list everything you know or think you know about the subject. If you get stuck, refer back to the photo you made. What do you know? What do you assume? What do you not know about the subject?" This is a great way to launch a new area of investigation.

Activity 112. Science Fair Projects

Include photos in science fair projects to document processes and record results. Display your photographs with student-written data, models, and experiments. Visitors see the "whole picture" when you document your research projects from beginning to end.

Activity 113. Picturing Machines

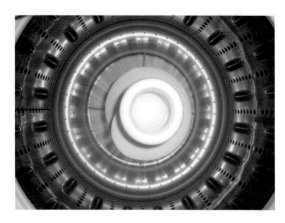

Have students make images of simple machines used at home and at school. Have them explain the work advantage of each machine. Alternatively, as a class project create a series of images that illustrate how the same task might be done without the machine.

Activity 114. Photo Problem Solving

Pose a problem like air pollution or solid waste disposal and collect photographic evidence of the problem and its causes. Have students sort through the photographic evidence in order to formulate a solution. "Create a display outside the classroom to share what you have learned with the rest of the school and community."

Activity 115. Good Health

Take photographs of students practicing good health and fitness habits. Have your class create a series of images that contrast the difference between good and bad health habits. Display these on a bulletin board as a constant reminder of good practices.

Activity 116. Weather Photos

Have students observe and photograph clouds each afternoon at the same time, such as 2:00. Collect the images and forecast the weather based on the cloud types. Save the images to share with subsequent classes. Use weather photographs to generate weather reports that can be presented in mock TV programs.

Activity 117. The Secret Building

Photograph elements of a building that are normally hidden. This might include duct works and wiring that run between the ceiling and the acoustic tile drop ceiling or basements that contain mechanical plants for buildings. Discuss what these things do and why they are necessary.

Activity 118. Instant Photo Processes

Use a developing Polaroid instant photograph as a focal point for brainstorming:

- Why are the colors emerging sequentially?
- What are the chemicals involved?
- Do other films develop the same way?
- Does temperature affect the developing process?
- How does light change the exposure?

Have the students call the technical information number (800-225-1618) or visit the Polaroid Web site (www.polaroid.com) to gain information.

Activity 119. Real Science

Begin with an image of an object. Ask students how they would start from scratch to create that object. "What raw materials and knowledge of physical process would be required to make that object? What tools would you need? What raw materials would you need to make the tools? Break everything down to its most basic component. Start with simple objects and progress to more complex objects."

Activity 120. Evidence Excursions

Send students with cameras to find evidence of concepts being studied in the classroom such as erosion, decomposition, seasonal change, and pollution. Have them add descriptions to their photographs and display them in team project posters or in journals.

Activity 121. Changing Light

"Photograph the same exterior scene at different times of the day. In addition to changes in shadows, are there changes in colors? Why? Discuss the different effects of light passing through the atmosphere at different angles."

Activity 122. Things I Don't Know

Ask students to make a list of scientific or mechanical objects or phenomena that they do not know. Have them narrow the list down to two or three clearly stated questions. Ask them to make photographs illustrating the subject of their questions. Have the class share the questions in research and discussion.

Activity 123. Imagine Science in the Future

Have each student make one photograph that represents a scientific skill that will be essential in the future. Have students write a short essay about why this skill will be important. Next, have students make an image that represents a branch of science that will be important in the future, but that does not currently exist (for example, creating artificial atmospheres for other planets).

Activity 124. Colored Light

Cut pieces of colored acetate large enough to cover camera lenses and flash units. "Try making pictures with the colored acetate covering the lens only. Then photograph the same subject with the acetate covering the flash unit only. Compare the images. How or why are they different? Make another image of an object indoors with flash. Photograph the same object indoors without flash. How are the pictures different? What does this tell you about light, or about the film used to record the light?"

Activity 125. Science Careers

Have students begin by making photographs that represent the careers they want to pursue. Have them use the images to write about the specific science knowledge someone in that profession might need. As a class, categorize the professions into high, medium, or low science knowledge professions. Make more photographs to fill in the categories. Discuss the differences.

Science

Activity 126. Energy Search

Have students photograph a variety of machines and living things, such as plants and animals, automobiles and trains. Post the images on a bulletin board and assign teams to find out what makes these things go. "Where do they get the energy to do what they do? What kind of fuel is required? Compare plants and animals to machines."

Activity 127. Objects in Motion

"Try tossing objects into the air and photographing them as they fall. Are the images clear or blurry? Try this several times using different objects of varying size and shapes. How are the images different? What might you guess about how a camera works from reviewing the results of these images?"

Activity 128. Famous Scientists

Have students research famous scientists and inventors and gather props and costume materials to have a photo made of themselves as their scientist. Try to have a distribution of different scientific disciplines such as chemistry, physics, biology, theory of evolution, astrophysics, mechanics, geology, genetics, and botany. Play a class game where you read the questions and students have to decide if their scientist would be a good person to answer that question. They do not actually need to answer the question; they just need to explain why they believe their scientist would know the answer.

ENVIRONMENTAL STUDIES

Activity 129. Biospheres

"Photograph ways we try to control our environment when we are indoors. This might include windows, air conditioning and heating systems, shades and curtains, fans, water heaters and coolers, insulation and sound proofing, carpeting, paint, and artwork. Discuss what you have discovered about the many ways we try to control our environment in our own little biosphere."

Activity 130. Resource Trails

"Photograph every point in and around your school where water comes in and goes out. Do the same thing for air. Make a trash trail: Follow trash from the student who creates it as far as you can." Display these images and discuss students' use or misuse of these resources.

Activity 131. Finders

Visit a field trip site in advance of the scheduled trip and photograph interesting details. Lay the images out four to a page and photocopy the pages. On the day of the field trip, distribute the pages and have students find and identify their objects.

Activity 132. Eco-Scavenger Hunt

Create a list of plants, animals, insects, or processes for students to find and photograph on a field trip, nature walk, or neighborhood safari. Assign point values for different items: the harder something is to find, the greater the point value. Back in the classroom, group the images by types and display them. Have  students analyze the photographs for details and record their observations in field or lab notebooks. Can items be categorized by appearance? Have them make some educated guesses about the things they photograph. Devise tests for determining whether their hypotheses are correct.

Environmental Studies

Activity 133. Weather Report

Start a class collection of weather photos. Try to get images of all different types of weather. Record the date, time, and location of each photograph on the front or back. Use the photos as weather flashcards. Assign a student the job of finding out the weather forecast for the next day. The following morning, let that student select and post the photo that illustrates the predicted weather. Collect images that document weather conditions that might indicate when tornados or other violent weather conditions are likely to occur.

Activity 134. Photo Calendar

Select a spot with an outside view and make one photograph of that spot every week during the school year. Try to include foliage and items that change. Record the date on each image and mount them on a horizontal calendar displayed in the classroom.

Activity 135. Photo Clock

Select a sunny day and photograph students outside on a cement or light-colored surface at different intervals during the day. Include the shadows in the viewfinder. Do not use the flash on the camera. Record the time each image is made on the back of each photograph. On the next sunny day, have students stand in the same positions of the photographs. Have them observe each other and the images and try to guess the time based on the shadows.

Activity 136. Imagine the Future

Each student takes two photographs that represent the following:

1. What might the worst environment of the future look like?

2. What might the best environment of the future look like?

Use these images as a springboard for discussion. "How might you work toward the best environment for the future?" As they proceed with environmental activities and projects, refer back to their original visual statements. Record both projected and actual goals as well.

Activity 137. Environment Study

Select a specific site to study. Research and photograph the various elements of the site, paying specific attention to the relationships found.

Photograph overall views as well as particular details. The final product can be in the form of reports or displays. Consider creating a web display. Put all the images up on a bulletin board and indicate the relationships by connecting the images with colored yarn and pushpins.

Activity 138. Biodiversity

Mark off an area to study with stakes and twine or natural boundaries like walls, streams, or walkways. The area can be as large or small as you choose. Send students out to identify various plants and animals. Every new form of life is recorded with photographs. How much diversity is present? Compare the diversity in different sites. Put the photos in plastic sleeves mounted to little wooden stakes. Use them as guides for nature walks organized by older students for younger students.

Activity 139. Economic Interdependence

Research and photograph businesses in the community. Examine the relationships between businesses and the environment. Look specifically for direct or indirect impacts that various businesses have on the environment. Create a bulletin board to chart and graph businesses based on their economic importance to the community, their necessity, and the amount of pollution or waste they generate. Discuss how political decisions that affect the environment are made.

Activity 140. Adopt a Community Treasure

Select a monument, park, or historical site. Work with the organization responsible to identify areas that need volunteer care. Design an appropriate strategy for addressing the needs of the site you select. Once you have identified the strategy, create "before" images that document the work you do. Maintain a timeline in class to show progress. Use your photos to create guidebooks to the site after your restoration work is complete. These can be photocopied and distributed to touring groups.

Activity 141. Living History

As a class or in teams students should create lists of interview questions about what their city or area used to be like. Have them use the public library as a resource for their research. After compiling the questions, ask students to interview senior members of the community. Record and photograph the interview subjects. Photograph specific sites or buildings discussed in the interviews. Create audiovisual archives about the community's past.

Environmental Studies

Activity 142. Waterways Project

"Trace the course of water that comes out of a tap or drinking fountain as far back as possible to its source. Follow its course as it leaves your classroom or school. Collect photographs of every distinct stage the water goes through on its journey. If you are unable to photograph an actual stage, make an image of something that symbolizes that stage. Create books or displays with photographs to share with other students." Discuss at what point each student has responsibility for how water is used.

Activity 143. Pollution Point of View

Have students select a plant or animal on which to focus their interest. Research and write stories about the plants or animals they have chosen. Illustrate the stories with images that show point of view. Encourage students to be creative in their search for effective points of view. What would bother a bird? What would a fish's view look like?

Activity 144. Campsite Camouflage

"At a park or wilderness preserve, identify areas or damages that show the impact of campers or excessive use. Work to make the site look as though no one had ever camped there to minimize the physical evidence of use. This can be done by dismantling fire rings, picking up trash, scattering cleared natural debris and brush, raking away footprints with downed branches, and so on. Document this process with before-and-after images. Create a display of the photographs for installation at the entrance to the park to help educate other campers."

Activity 145. Enviro-Links

Form photo pen-pal links with schools that share environmental concerns. Perhaps other schools are located along a coast of waterway or border an urban or national park. Exchange student letters and photographs depicting common environmental concerns. Display a map in the classroom. Post images as focal points for developing joint strategies to address shared concerns. Make photocopies of the photographs to use in joint proposals to local governments.

Activity 146. Endangered Views

"Select an historic building, a park, or natural site that is in danger of being lost or destroyed. Document the site with photographs. Determine whether the site is worth saving. Use these images to take polls in neighborhoods. Create photo flyers to raise support for action to save the endangered site. Use sketches along with the photographs to show what the restored site might look like."

Activity 147. Special Places

Many cultures believe that certain sites are sacred. Discuss the qualities a sacred site might have. Ask students to find and photograph their special places. Ask them what makes their site special. What do they feel when they visit the site? Do other students feel the same? Install a photo exhibit to bring attention to the importance of the special places.

Activity 148. Planting Project

Organize a tree-, shrub-, or flower-planting campaign. Contact local officials who can help you identify sites that might be enhanced by an organized planting program. Have students keep journals to record their personal commitment and record the planting they have done. Lead and motivate others by setting an example.

Activity 149. People in Power

Identify, interview, and photograph people in power who make environmental policy and decisions for local and national government. Keep charts and graphs to record their votes and opinions on key environmental issues. Use the chart to identify who should receive letters when you want to voice concerns. Display student charts so other students can learn how to voice their opinions.

Activity 150. The Power of Pictures

Observe and evaluate local environments. Identify environmental hot spots. Make images of these hot spots and use the photos to document or create focal points for photo petition drives or letter-writing campaigns. Photographs can be worth a thousand words. Create a wall chart of hot spots.

Environmental Studies

Activity 151. Patterns of Nature

"Photograph several solitary elements in natural or man-made settings that emphasize color, pattern, shape, or size. Create a photographic mural by arranging the photos in grid patterns. Pay attention to which images touch each other. How do they react to each other? Do they make larger patterns? If possible, make multiple images of the same patterns so that you can use repetition as an element of your composition." Assign a new pattern artist on a regular basis to rearrange the images and create new murals.

Activity 152. Flower Painting

"Plan a wildflower garden by photographing a site that could benefit from a splash of natural color. Attach the photo to a larger sheet of paper and draw, paint, or color in the flowers as they will look when they bloom. Expand the image off the photograph and onto the page. Experiment with different materials such as fabric paints, sequins, colored glue, or even natural materials in a collage over the photo."

SOCIAL STUDIES

Activity 153. Self-Profile

Discuss various aspects of identity and design a common format for student profiles. Profiles might elicit information about age, goals, religion, friends, likes and dislikes, interests, favorite books, nationalities, professions, or education. "Examine photographs from books or magazines and discuss how the images reveal or conceal identity." Have students complete their own profiles. Plan a profile photograph. Pair up students and have them take a photo to go with their profiles.

Activity 154. Neighbors (for ELL students)

"Visit with and photograph a neighbor who was born in this country. Discuss topics that might be considered sensitive in this country such as money, salary, social class, sex, age, marital status, and health. Write down any expressions that seem odd to you. Bring the images and your notes back to class for presentation and discussion. Photograph people from your own country in the environments they have created for themselves here. How are they different or similar to the photos you took of natives?"

Activity 155. Field Trip to America (for ELL students)

"Document a public place or event with an eye toward its American distinction. Photograph events or occasions that display cultural characteristics. Photograph features you consider to be uniquely American. Discuss the images. Trace where these elements originated. What makes them American? Can you determine if these traditions came from another culture? Display the images with your findings."

Social Studies

Activity 156. Time of Day

"Choose a particular time of day and photograph activities and themes. Discuss the images. What is happening in the photos? How universal is this usage of time? Where would we find these things occurring? Where would we not find them occurring? Expand the discussion to include alternative activities that might occur at that particular time of day." Have students write about their findings and present them to the class.

Activity 157. How To

"Look at 'How To' books such as cookbooks, assembly instructions, directions, and so on." Some people rely more on photos or drawings, while other people get their information from text. Ask students about their individual preferences. "Create a text and a series of images that demonstrate how to do something. Try to select topics that not everyone knows how to do. Examine the results. Share them with others and see how clearly they communicate. Ask people whether the images or text was most helpful, or perhaps the combination."

Activity 158. Getting Around

Discuss ways to get from one place to another using various forms of transportation. Using photographs, document a trip that shows location, sights, mode of transportation, advantages and disadvantages of that mode of transportation, and its alternatives. How is transportation different in other areas of the country or world?

Activity 159. Tourist Guide

"Prepare a guide to your community. Discuss what to include. Photograph and gather information about the places students have decided to include. Compile them into books to photocopy and distribute to new students. How might a guidebook be different if it was intended for someone new to the United States?"

Activity 160. On the Job

"Photograph and interview people at their jobs. What do they do? Can we tell what they do by their uniforms or tools? Make an oral or written presentation to accompany your photographs. Make a poster showing what to do or not to do when applying for a job."

Activity 161. City Spaces

"Identify open city spaces. Photograph various activities that occur in those spaces. Develop broader categories such as relaxation, business, romance, eating, exercise, and so on, to organize the activities you have photographed. Write descriptions of what is happening in the images. Discuss whether the use of open spaces was planned or happened spontaneously. Are some uses of open spaces better than other uses? Why?"

Activity 162. Photo Funnies (for ELL students)

Discuss problems that might be caused by misunderstanding due to pronunciation or accent. Make a list of word pairs easily confused such as stink/sting, eel/heel, feel/veal, three/tree, chip/cheap, and piece/peas. What are some situations where error in pronunciation could cause problems? Plan and photograph a story about miscommunication. Write the dialogue on nametags to be cut out in the shape of dialogue balloons and stuck directly on the image.

Activity 163. Before and After

Discuss products that might be appropriate for before-and-after advertisements (shampoo, mouthwash, perfume, fertilizer, language learning course, car, detergent). Look at before-and-after ads from magazines and newspapers. "During one evening of television viewing, record the number of commercials that use this approach to advertise their product. What percentage of the commercials do this? Design an advertisement with text and before-and-after photos for a product of your choice. Do a before-and-after advertisement for staying in school and getting an education."

Activity 164. Disguises

Discuss ways of hiding identity with a camera. This might include abstraction, shadow, silhouettes, association, or blurring. Make photographs hiding the identity or people, places, or things known to the class. Pass the images around and allow students to ask yes/no questions to guess the true identity of the subject.

Activity 165. Picture Postcards

Discuss the customary use of postcards. "Who receives postcards? To whom would you not send a postcard? What sort of things would you or would you not write on a postcard? What sort of pictures do you generally

Social Studies

see on postcards?" Have students make their own picture postcard by making a photograph and writing a message on the back. Discuss how you would send a postcard to a student in another country. "Should you write in their language or yours? How would you feel about receiving a postcard written in a foreign language?"

Activity 166. Brand X Men/Women

Discuss with the class the makeup of an ideal person. In a perfect world, what would a perfect person look like? List various adjectives that relate to this perfect person. Using a long white sheet of paper, trace the outline of one of the students. Ask each student to make a photograph of a perfect hand, leg, face, hairstyle, foot, and so on. Add these images to the outline to build the perfect person. Now have students study advertising that claims to improve or affect the various parts of the body they have photographed. Photograph the products or bring in advertisements and attach them to the perfect person poster. Discuss our visions of beauty and perfection.

Activity 167. What Are Dreams Made Of?

We all dream of a better world. Have each student make an image that communicates his or her own dream for a better world. Have the class discuss or write about each image. Discuss what can be done to make some of these dreams a reality. Before students share explanations of the photos, post them all on the bulletin board and ask students to interpret the photos. Ask them how clearly the photographs communicate the dreams.

Activity 168. Dream Jobs

Make images of various people doing their jobs. Discuss the various occupations. Make a chart of positive and negative aspects to different occupations. Create different categories to organize the jobs by pay scale, degree requirement, full or part time, or physical requirements. Discuss how personal these value judgments are. Have students create and present their own idea of a dream job. Have them photograph themselves in their dream jobs.

Social Studies

Activity 169. Time Capsule

Have students each make one or more photographs to be included in a time capsule. The theme might be "What I want the future to know about or remember from my time." Have students include written explanations of what they have chosen to include. Post these time capsule images on the wall and discuss them prior to burial.

Activity 170. Legacy Wall

Have each graduating fifth-, eighth-, or twelfth-grade student make a single image that represents, depicts, or symbolizes their favorite person, place, activity, or thing in the school. Select a large wall in the cafeteria or other public location. Post each student's photograph next to one another with the student's name and graduation year clearly marked. Grow the "legacy wall" in a yearly ceremony that adds the next graduating class. Consider adding an essay contest that would accompany each image. If people are honored on the "legacy wall," celebrate them at the yearly ceremony.

Activity 171. Student/Senior Histories

Have students use cameras and tape recorders to interview senior volunteers about their memories of childhood, community, historical events, and so on. Before doing the interviews, have students prepare lists of good interview questions and practice interviewing techniques on each other. It may help to have younger students work in teams and share the responsibility for interviewing, photographing, and recording. Back in the classroom, transcribe oral histories into books or posters. Remember to share the results with the interview subjects.

Activity 172. Photo Interview

Have students create images of landmarks and people to use as aids for senior interviews. People find it easy to talk about photos; they often trigger memories of how things used to be. Photos can be used to prompt interview subjects to elaborate and reminisce. Create a timeline in the classroom to get a sense of what events were occurring when their subjects were born, were children, were teenagers, got married, began a family, and so on.

Activity 173. Points of Origin

Post a map on the wall. Photograph all students and have them ask their parents and grandparents their place of origin. Encourage students to go back as far as possible in their family history. Post photographs around the map using yarn and pushpins to link images to countries or origin. Have students research the country and geographical regions.

Activity 174. Neighborhood Life Cycle

Create a graph of squares the size of photographs. Along the top, list the categories: public place, structure, landscape, vehicles, and streetscapes. Down the side, list the categories: historic or old, new, in progress, refurbished, deteriorated, and personalized. Illustrate each block of the grid with an image showing an example of the elements that intersect with it.

Activity 175. Thematic Area Guides and Maps

Select a theme such as important jobs in the community and make a map or community guide with photos showing where those jobs take place. Photograph fire stations, police precinct stations, and hospitals. Place them on a map showing their location. Does everyone have an emergency facility nearby? Photograph distinctive examples of architecture in the area. Place the photos on maps to locate them. Create an area tour guide of unusual architecture.

Activity 176. Awareness Board

Have students sit in silence with eyes closed, listening and then writing down a list of sounds they have never noticed before. Give each student an opportunity to photograph one of the things on their list. Make an "Awareness Board" to display the newly discovered things. Stress that there is always something new to learn. This can also be done as a homework assignment by having students find and list ten new discoveries at home. Add those images to the "Awareness Boards" as well.

Activity 177. Interdependence Day

Have students create lists of relationships that exist in their world. These should be examples of interdependency and cooperative activity. The more basic the list, the better (farmers' crops to the store to the kitchen table, or fuel to the car to going on vacation). Make images that illustrate this list. Discuss and illustrate with photo examples situations where cooperation would be a real asset but is lacking.

Activity 178. Bill of Rights

Have students select a freedom guaranteed in the Bill of Rights and make a photograph of something in their world that would be different if that freedom was not assured. Have them make images of freedoms that are in the Bill of Rights, but that seem to be threatened.

Activity 179. Culture Cards

Make a photograph that represents a culture. Attach that image to a card with room to write notes about customs, arts, foods, clothing, religion, and so on. Create culture cards for every culture represented in the class. Expand to create culture cards for cultures in your area, state, region, country, and part of the world.

Activity 180. Elements of Culture

Discuss objects that form elements of culture. Photograph common objects from the list and describe what cultures and circumstances brought those objects to America. Create a bulletin board of common cultural elements.

Activity 181. Cultural Reporter

"Photograph a cultural event such as Native American dances, St. Patrick's Day parades, Scottish Clan gatherings, Cinco de Mayo celebrations, Kwanzaa, or Chinese New Year. Write descriptive paragraphs to accompany the images. Research the roots and elements of these celebrations."

Activity 182. Places We Live

"Photograph things that are unique to an area or which tend to differentiate where we are (steer, cactus, snow, mountains, Statue of Liberty, palm tree, and so on). Also photograph things that might be found anywhere (fast food restaurants, cars, televisions). Discuss how people from different areas might react differently to seeing these things. Make images of things that require certain environments to be useful."

Social Studies

Activity 183. Historic Photos

"Select a period from history and find images that represent it. Discuss why the photos look the way they do. Assemble costumes and props and try to recreate the images as authentically as possible. Before shooting the picture, look for give-away signs that make the image appear contemporary."

Activity 184. Technology Chains

Select a general field of human endeavor and photograph examples of early-to-recent technological innovations such as charred wooden sticks to charcoal to pencils to pens to printing presses to typewriters to word processors to computers. Display these technology chains on the bulletin board. Create technology chains for transportation, medicine, image making, clothing, heating food, and so on. Discuss technologies that have positive as well as negative effects on cultures.

Activity 185. Imports and Exports

Gather and photograph items that are made, wholly or in part, in other countries. Discuss why they are made in other countries. Photograph a group of products that are made locally that you think would make strong exports to another country. Have students target and research a specific country to export to and then prepare a report or presentation that explains why these products should be exported to another country.

Activity 186. Photographs in Democracies

Discuss how important visuals are in our culture and how they are now linked to the democratic process. Ask students if they believe people are elected on the basis of how they look. Ask them how it might be different if they had to choose between candidates they could not see. How would they make a decision? Ask students how race, gender, physical condition, or different personal challenges affect the election process. Have students create election posters with photographs of themselves as candidates.

Activity 187. Photo Pen Pals

"Establish photo pen pals with students in a school in another country or different part of the United States. Compare environments, opportunities, daily routines, and so on." Post the pen-pal photos on a bulletin board accompanied by written descriptions and personal letters.

Activity 188. Friends

Discuss the importance of friendship. Have students pose and photograph each other. Record information about the subject's physical description, biographical sketch, tastes, opinions, and favorite activities. Photocopy the images and information. Create a "friend book" to take home. Locate residences on a map and place photographs in appropriate spots.

Activity 189. Neighborhood Map

Photograph people, places, and things that make up a neighborhood. Make a large street map of the neighborhood. Label it with street names and directions. Position the photographs on the map in appropriate locations. Consider expanding the map into a 3-D model by gluing the images onto blocks. Investigate the architecture of the buildings in the photographs.

Activity 190. Public Officials

"Select public officials to interview and photograph. Plan in advance by learning about the jobs and positions of the public officials you select. Bring the photographs back to class for a presentation. Develop a hierarchy of public positions based on the images. Who reports to whom? Which are the most powerful positions in the community?"

Activity 191. Facades

"Photograph different types of buildings in the area and record the age, use, and style of each. In class, display the images together and compare them. Photograph the front and back of each building. How do they compare? Sequence the photographs according to age. How have the styles and materials used to build the structures changed through the years?"

Activity 192. Signs

Photograph various types of signs such as street signs, public signs, emergency signs, and advertising signs. Display and discuss the images. How many different uses for signs were found? Why are signs designed and shaped the way they are? What similarities do all signs share? How do new signs and old signs compare?

Social Studies

Activity 193. Patterns of Growth

"Select a street that runs from the center of town to the edge of the town's boundaries. Photograph the buildings along the street at regular intervals. Arrange the images on a map and discuss how they change. What patterns do you see? Do these patterns suggest values or needs of the community? Try mapping the growth of residential, business, and industrial areas."

Activity 194. Leisure Time

Discuss the things we do with our leisure time. Does everybody in the class do the same things? Do we do different things at different times of the year? Photograph some of the various leisure activities discussed. How are these activities different in other cultures?

Activity 195. Then and Now

"Research and collect old photographs of your town and community. Make new images from the same point of view as the original photos. What changes are evident? What brought about these changes? Do you think the changes have been for the better? Locate the new and old photos on a map." Invite people who remember the area to talk about it using the map made by the students.

Activity 196. Landmarks

Discuss what constitutes a landmark. Talk about local landmarks and their history. How does something become a landmark? Photograph landmarks in the area. Create maps with the images of the landmarks as markers. Research the chosen landmarks. Are there things that are not considered landmarks that you feel should be?

Activity 197. Criminal Justice

Discuss what happens when a crime is committed. List the steps that occur from investigation to arrest, arraignment to exoneration or conviction, and sentencing. Make photographs to represent each of the steps.

Post these as a display in the classroom. "Interview and photograph people who play key roles in the process such as police officers, judges, bondspersons, lawyers, juries, and wardens."

Activity 198. Religion and the Community

Make images of religious buildings and related activities in the community. Group the photographs according to denomination. Sequence them according to building age. Research past and present relationships of the building to the community.

Activity 199. Ages and Stages

Discuss the stages of human development. Photograph examples of infant, toddler, school age, teen, young adult, adult, and senior. Discuss and write about milestone events that may occur during these developmental stages such as baptism, science fair award, sweet sixteen, college, occupation, raising a family, or retirement.

Activity 200. Gender Roles

Discuss gender roles that are endorsed, formally or informally, by the culture in which you live. Photograph men and women in both traditional and nontraditional gender roles. What differences in current beliefs about gender roles can be observed from old photographs and advertisements? What roles have changed the most from the past?

Activity 201. Attitudes Toward Death

Make arrangements to photograph various elements of a cemetery. Explore the grounds and discuss the many dates found on headstones. Discuss periods in history and what roles people have had in the past: father, mother, mayor, builder, artist, and so on.

Social Studies

Activity 202. Economic Interdependence

Photograph and analyze one or more aspects of a specific business enterprise. Discuss in detail the economics apparent within the photographs. Mount the images and draw lines of economic interdependence. Make images that reveal the tangible economic forces on society.

Activity 203. My House

Allow students to check out a camera to photograph their homes. Discuss characteristics that all homes have in common. What are some of these features? Construct a grid or graph and organize home photos by category: apartment, condominium, townhouse, detached house, one story, two story, ranch, colonial, and so on.

Activity 204. School Maps

Create a large bulletin board floor plan of the school. Make photographs of features and locations in the school and add them to the map as markers. Display this map in the lobby for visitors and new students.

Activity 205. Local Businesses

Arrange to visit a local business and document with photographs and interviews how the business is operated. Create a photo essay on poster board to highlight the product or service the business provides. Include images of owners, managers, and employees. When the project is complete, display the results at the business location.

Activity 206. Local History

Create local history displays featuring photographs of natural and manmade landmarks. Have a local history dress-up day. Photograph students in costumes that represent the ethnicity, religion, occupations, politicians, and so on. Add the images to the display.

Activity 207. Timelines

"Create a timeline by making photographs that represent specific dates. This might include photos of a person born in 1910, a building built in 1915, a park created in 1920, a vehicle manufactured in 1925, a book published in 1930, and so on. The more dates you attempt to fill, the better the challenge. Extend the timeline into the future by doing artwork that illustrates things, people, and events in the future."

Activity 208. The Day the Earth Stood Still

"Imagine that you are about to be taken away on an alien spaceship to a distant planet. You may never return to Earth. You are allowed to make one photograph as a lasting reminder of what you left behind. The purpose of the photograph is two-fold. It will serve as your personal reminder of what you left behind and it may be requested by the alien scientists to study Earth." Have students take their picture and explain to a partner why they chose that subject.

Activity 209. Culture Maps

Focus on a particular ethnic group and gather photographs of objects, architecture, art, music, food, and fashion that represent the culture. Create a museum-style display of these things. Describe what impact this subculture has had on the larger culture.

Activity 210. Memorial Days

Discuss memorial statues, commemorative plaques, objects, and places. Have each student select a subject for his or her personal memorial (something they would like to see remembered by others). Have them make a photograph of something that could contribute to the memorial.

ARTS AND HUMANITIES

Activity 211. The Color of Light

"Select a scene outdoors to photograph. Make an image from the same location in early morning, at noon, and late in the afternoon. How are the colors different in each photograph? Why are the colors different? Photograph a textured surface under different lighting conditions. Which one makes the surface look more three-dimensional?"

Activity 212. Blind Landscapes

Divide the class so that each student has a partner. One member of each pair makes an image of a particular scene. Without showing the image to their partner, they decode, or describe the photo in detail. Based on this description, the partner then draws the image. Once both partners have had the opportunity to photograph and draw, display the drawings next to the photos.

Activity 213. Emotional Colors

"Select emotions and associate colors to the emotions. Make images that depict the feeling tone reflected in the color." Choose a student as a model to pose in front of different colored backdrops. "Do the different colors change the feeling tone of each image?" What colors do students associate with feelings of happiness, sadness, and fear?

Activity 214. Height, Perspective, and Distance

Discuss the concept of distance and perspective. "If you look at a tree in the distance and gradually move closer to it, how does the appearance of its size change? What happens to the appearance of two objects that are the same size at different distances? Photograph a person and a tree and make it appear that the person is larger than the tree. Make a class photograph in which everyone appears to be the exact same height."

Activity 215. Artists

"Interview and photograph artists in their studios or workspaces. What do the images reveal about the artists? Are there any similar characteristics between the artists?" Discuss the role of artists in society. "Try to compose a photograph that best represents the way an artist creates."

Activity 216. Color Wheels

Ask students to make photographs with strong colors that make up the majority of the image. Once everyone has a photograph, organize the images into color charts of red, orange, yellow, green, blue, indigo, and violet. Have students hold their photos and form a circle that reflects the order in the color wheel.

Activity 217. CD Cover

Look at musical CD covers and discuss the relationship of the imagery to the music. Ask students to create a photograph for a CD that conveys a sense of the content of the music. Scan the image into a computer and integrate text into the image to reflect the CD title.

Activity 218. Portraits, Light, and Shadow

Set up a natural-light portrait studio outdoors. Supply students with aluminum foil and large sheets of white and colored cardboard to reflect sunlight onto a model. Try cutting small circles out of large sheets of cardboard and having students hold them between the sun and the subject at varying distances. Can they create natural spotlights? Take all photos without flash so that the changes in lighting will be obvious. Discuss the results.

Activity 219. Photo Expansion

"Glue a photograph to a large sheet of construction paper. Use crayons, markers, or paints to expand the photo to the edges of the paper. Consider allowing the photograph to stand out by doing the expanded drawing in monochromatic media."

Activity 220. Seeing Out, Seeing In

Discuss the difference between windows and mirrors. Have students make two photographs, one as a metaphor of a window of the world and the other as a metaphor of a mirror reflecting oneself. Have the students write about the images.

Activity 221. Emulsion Drawing

Have students collect a blunt pointed tool that will allow them to apply firm pressure. Clay modeling tools work well, as do wood styluses. Younger students can use frozen treat sticks or ballpoint pen caps. As soon as the instant photograph ejects from the camera, place it on a hard surface and begin to draw directly on it using firm pressure. The lines drawn part the emulsion of the film and the light reacts in a way that makes the lines permanent. Drawing at different times during the development and with varying degrees of pressure will create different colored lines.

Activity 222. Panoramas

"While standing in a fixed position, make a series of images that slightly overlap each other. Pay close attention to what is in the edge of the viewfinder of each photograph. The panoramas can be horizontal or vertical. Tape the photos together to create one long or tall image. Try making one long image that represents a 360° view."

Activity 223. Photo Sounds

"Photograph inanimate objects, either manufactured or natural. Assign sounds to each image. This can be a sound made with an instrument, object, or human voice. Record the sounds to coincide with the images. Try composing a song of sounds based on the order of the photos."

Activity 224. Surface Drawing

"Use permanent markers and paint pens to draw on photographs. Fabric or puff paints can be used for a nice three-dimensional effect. Spray the finished images with a fixative or hairspray."

Activity 225. Photo Ornaments

Photograph the front and back of each student. "Glue the images together. Punch a hole at the top of pictures and attach a ribbon with an ornament hanger. When they spin both sides of the student can be seen. Decorate the edges of the photographs with paint, glitter, or ribbon pieces. These make nice ornaments and holiday gifts."

Activity 226. Photo Mobiles

Pick a theme and have students create images based on the theme. "Tape photographs together back-to-back or attach photos to shapes made from cardboard. Suspend the shapes from wire hangers to make mobiles."

Activity 227. Photo Puzzles

"Make an enlarged photocopy of a photograph. Cut the enlargement into several small squares. Mix up the squares and reassemble the image like a puzzle."

Activity 228. Photo Totem Pole

Attach a dowel rod or curtain pole to a base that can be attached to the floor or weighted so as not to tip over. Have each student make four images that represent a theme. Tape the images together to form cubes without a top or bottom. Slide them over the dowel rod and stack them to create a group totem pole.

Activity 229. Fun Photos

Assign students in pairs to devise a photo where it appears as though they have two heads, four arms, or three legs. "Try to make the photographs as realistic as possible. Use large clothing and other props. Write a story about a mythical creature to be displayed with the images."

Activity 230. Photo Bookmarks

Have students create their own photo bookmarks that celebrate an aspect of reading. Give students a theme such as "I get lost in books!" or "Do not disturb—I'm on a mental field trip." After they make their images, use permanent markers to label the photos "This book is being read by _____."

Activity 231. Photo Project Documents

Some art projects require many steps and extended time to complete. Use photographs to document the progression of the project. These images will help students to see progress and document the creative process. They can also motivate students to complete projects.

Arts and Humanities

Activity 232. Photo Cards

Photographs can be great starting points for greeting cards for holidays, birthdays, and special events during the year. They also make nice gifts to parents.

Activity 233. Photo Enlargements

Select a photograph and cover it with a sheet of clear plastic. Divide the picture space into small squares to form a grid. Give each student a square sheet of paper and have him or her enlarge one of the squares to the full size of the sheet of paper. This will require an extended period to complete. When all the sections are complete, attach them to form a single large image.

Activity 234. Custom Coloring Books

Use a photocopy machine to enlarge a class picture to a full sheet of paper. Using paint, markers, colored pencils, and crayons, have learners hand-color the images. Put all the individual pictures into one class book.

Activity 235. Symbols and Stories

Different styles of music portray different stories: the blues, folk, bluegrass, rock and roll, and even classical music all tell stories. "Listen to a track on the CD and write a fictitious story. Take four photos that could illustrate the story. Using a musical selection as the soundtrack, play the music in the background as the story is read and the photos are shared."

Activity 236. Tune In and Just Do It

"Listen to a track on a CD. Make this song symbolic by finding creative or metaphoric ways to relate it to classroom/school events. Have the students decide what symbols best represent this song and make representational photos."

Activity 237. From the Street to the Sheet

Much like graffiti, music has a subliminal influence. Discuss the music played in the grocery store or an elevator or in a dentist's waiting room. "Make photos of areas and situations that could benefit from the subliminal influences of music (such as noisy cafeterias). Select various tracks from the CDs to coincide with the photos." Have the students submit the audiovisual packet to the principal in the form of a proposal or request to begin playing music in the areas depicted in the photos. "Monitor the effects of the music through photos and anecdotal documentation."

Activity 238. Musical Association

Music often reminds us of holidays, events, or even moments in our personal histories. Choose tracks from the CDs to be used specifically for different subjects throughout the course of the school day. Display visual learning activity photos shot during each subject's lessons. At the end of each week, play the tracks as an auditory cue and have the students select the photographs from the lessons. This is a helpful and fun way to review the subject goals of the week.

Activity 239. Musical to Visual Culture

"Listen to a track on a CD. Discuss what culture comes to mind from the style of the music. Take photos of people, clothing, and various items that relate to that culture."

Activity 240. Yin and Yang

"Identify and discuss opposing music (such as music from a merry-go-round versus music from a suspenseful movie). Find two tracks on a CD that oppose each other and take photos to illustrate their opposing and imposing effects."

Activity 241. Stones to Bones

Dance is a series of steps or body movements. Have the students choose a track from a CD and choreograph their own steps, then use photos to document the steps necessary to learn the dance. The product will be a visual "how to" manual for their new dance.

Activity 242. Natural Prisms

Focusing on the elements in music is an important way to enhance the students' perception of what they hear in a song. "After listening to a track on a CD, identify the instruments that are being used and which musical instrument family they belong to." Have students take photos to represent what they have learned (a photo of a tree blowing in the wind represents the woodwind family; a photo of the custodian's hammer or an old-fashioned school bell represents the percussion family).

Activity 243. Rainbow Windows

Color can alter mood just as it can alter images. Discuss color therapy, and why walls (hospitals, prisons, cafeterias, and so on) are painted in certain colors. Music therapy is used much in the same way. Ask children to assign color to the music on a CD and make photos to represent the changes, and then to articulate why they chose the color (such as, "this music is green because it makes me feel like I'm watching the swaying trees in the summer breeze").

Activity 244. Musical Mosaic

Much of music is written in sequential patterns. For example, a 4/4 time signature indicates there are four beats to a measure and the quarter note gets the beat. Have the students make photos of three-dimensional items that illustrate time signatures. "Photograph a brick wall and highlight four bricks in a row coloring three in one color and the fourth in another color to represent a 3/4 time signature."

Activity 245. The Art of Exclusion

Music is the art of diversion. Have the students listen to the introduction of a CD, then stop the music. Ask them to describe how they think the song will continue. Now finish the piece. Have the students make photos of partial objects that might be diversions to the actual object (such as a photo of a shoe on the playground: Does this imply someone is running around barefoot? Could it be that a student slipped it off for a moment to shake out a pebble?).

Activity 246. Optic Tricks

Play a track from a CD through a headset. Hold the headset across the room from the student. Ask students to close their eyes and listen carefully. Every five seconds, take one step closer to the student until you have moved close enough to place the headset over the student's ears. "Do the same with photos. Shoot a series of photos, first from faraway, then shooting closer, then closer. Use the visual imagery to describe the experience felt earlier with the headset."

Activity 247. Take a Bite

Divide the class into two groups, Group A and Group B. Using a tape recorder, have Group A record five-second sound bites from each track on a CD, then have Group B create a photo representing each sound bite. Next, have Group B sequence the sound bites to create a new song and have Group A follow the same sequence using the photos to create a new story.

EARLY CHILDHOOD

Activity 248. Photo Expectations

Make photographs that are visual representations of classroom rules and expectations. Use students in the images demonstrating appropriate classroom behaviors and duties. Post them in an area where they will serve as a constant reminder of positive things in the classroom.

Activity 249. People and Uniforms

Discuss the use and purpose of uniforms. Talk about the people who wear them and the services they provide. Make close-up photographs of each student and mount them on individual pieces of construction paper. Cut out pictures of people in uniforms from magazines and newspapers and paste them over the images of the students so that it appears as though the students were wearing the uniforms. Ask the students to choose the uniforms they would most like to wear and discuss their choices.

Activity 250. Photo Places

Students learn better in a learning environment that is well organized. Make photographs of each student to use as markers as to where they are to hang their coats, store their lunches, or put their backpacks. Be sure to write the student's name on his or her photo.

Activity 251. Photo Lotto

Make a list of concepts or themes you are teaching. Make duplicate photographs to coincide with objects from the lessons (seasons, types of transportation, machines, living things, and so on). Mount one of the images on a poster board and distribute the duplicates to the students. Have them match their photograph to the original on the board and identify the object from what is being taught.

Activity 252. Concentration Game

Make two photographs of the same objects around the school such as toys, books, desks, or crayons. Shuffle the images and place them face down on a table. Take turns turning them over in search of a match. If a match is made, the student collects the images. The student with the most pairs wins!

Activity 253. Groups

Collect groups of objects that share similarities, such as function, color, shape, size, or initial consonant sound. Have students examine the images looking for similarities as well as objects that could be in other groups.

Activity 254. Photo Bingo

Using poster board, create bingo game cards with consonants in the grids. Give students markers such as poker chips or buttons. Display a photograph of an object asking students to identify the initial consonant sound and locate the letter on the bingo card that represents that sound.

Activity 255. Spatial Relationships

Have students pose for images of various positions: standing ON a box, sitting UNDER a table, jumping OVER a toy, standing BETWEEN two students, and so on.

Activity 256. Photo Peek-A-Boo

Make photographs of objects and people that students will easily recognize. Mount the images on tag board behind paper doors that will reveal a small portion of the photo. Have students try to guess what the image is based on the clue behind the door.

Activity 257. Learning Centers

Photograph learning centers in the classroom. Create a photo pocket with each student's name; arrange them on a bulletin board. At center time, have students take turns putting the photo of the chosen center into their photo pockets. The number of photos of each learning center will help to ensure the appropriate number of students in that center at any given time.

Early Childhood

Activity 258. Basic Shapes

Discuss the basic group of shapes (square, rectangle, circle, and triangle). Have students identify things in the classroom and school that have these basic shape properties. Make images of these objects. Have students lay tracing paper over the photos and trace the objects.

Activity 259. Sequences

Make images of a series of steps needed to complete a task, such as a recipe. Discuss what would happen if the steps were out of order. After the activity is completed, shuffle the images and have the students put them in sequential order.

Activity 260. Weather Reports

Create a class collection of images depicting various types of weather. Record the date, time, and location of each photograph. Ask students to predict weather for the following day by selecting an image.

Activity 261. Times of Day

Create a large poster with a drawing of a clock in its center. Make two clock hands and attach them to the clock with a thumbtack or brad. Place images around the clock of activities that occur at various times of the day.

Activity 262. Class Documentation

Use photographs to document positive student behavior or accomplishments. These make excellent images for permanent records and communication between home and school.

Activity 263. Day Care Chart

Use images of students attached to individual clipboards to keep their charts quickly and easily identifiable. This is also a great aid to substitutes to know which students are present, and to identify students by their names.

PORTFOLIOS

Activity 264. Meet the Storyteller

Have students create a book about their life. On the front cover, include an intriguing title, a photograph, and the author's (storyteller's) name. Inside the front cover should be a brief description of the story. Inside the back cover should be a photograph of the storyteller, along with some interesting facts to draw the reader into the story. On the back cover should be a metaphorical image of the storyteller, an explanation of the image, and quotes from those who know the storyteller.

Activity 265. Portfolio Photos

Before students create images for their portfolios, ask "What is the story you wish to tell? What is the setting of the story? Who are the characters in the story? What are the important objects of the story? What scene or moment of action will be shown?"

Activity 266. Photo Cards

"Create photo cards to be used for photographic annotation and glue them to the back of images. The cards should contain the following information: Who or what is the photo of? When was the photo taken? Where was the photo taken? What is happening in the photo? Why was the photo taken? How does this photo portray the real event?"

Activity 267. Photo Journals

Have students take their own photos illustrating personal accomplishments (in or out of school). Ask them to attach their pictures to a photo journal page and annotate. This will build self-esteem and provide insight about a student's interests.

Portfolios

Activity 268. Decoding Photos

Form students into groups. Have one member from each group photograph something of interest in or near the room. Circulate the image among group members. Each member should note something different in the photo until the visual content has been exhausted.

Activity 269. Reading Pictures

Ask students for factual observations from a photograph, such as "The car is red, I see two tires, and there is a tree behind the car." Then, while passing around the image, ask students for embellishment to factual observations, such as "The car is new (because it is so shiny)," "it has four tires (even though only two are visible)," and "it is winter (because the tree is bare)."

Activity 270. Photo Exploration

Have students examine images and brainstorm themes that might link them together. Possibilities might include the similar or disparate angles from which the photographs were taken.

Activity 271. Photo Relationships

Form the class into teams. After discussing the various factors that might relate one image to another, have each team agree on a theme for their photographic series. Each student should then take a photograph consistent with the theme of his or her group. Display each team's series and challenge the other teams to find the linking factor.

Activity 272. Photo Storytelling

Select three random photographs and have students create a story. Weave a narrative based on individual interpretations of the visual information contained in each image.

Activity 273. Creating a Visual Story

Form the class into a large circle. Distribute unrelated images. Have the first student begin a story based on the visual information in his or her photograph, then have the next student continue the story based on his or her image, and so on. Audiotaping or video-taping this process showcases student creativity, provides an opportunity to critique ideas, and establishes a reference for building sequels or new stories. A variation could be to have small groups or individual students create more than one narrative or written composition from the same images.

Activity 274. Visual Intelligences

Have students create photographic examples of Howard Gardner's multiple intelligences:

1. Linguistic (stories of reading, writing, words, and language);

2. Kinesthetic (stories of the body, its ability to move, perform complex tasks, and express thought and feeling);

3. Mathematic (stories of numbers, formulas, and computations);

4. Spatial (stories told with images, symbols, and the manipulation of objects in space);

5. Musical (stories of sound, tone, rhythm, and harmony);

6. Interpersonal (stories of social communication and interaction); Intrapersonal (stories of our deepest selves); and

7. Naturalist (stories of our interaction with nature and societal patterns).

Activity 275. Photo Poems

Have students make images without people in them. Pair students and have them collaborate on a poem using the two images. Then have students photograph family and friends and write poems about the subjects' best characteristics.

Activity 276. Image-inary Tales

"Photograph a family member. Trade images and write humorous stories about the person in the picture. Share the stories and have other students embellish them."

Activity 277. Visual Grammar

"Use photographs to generate lists of verbs or nouns. Look up the words and write down definitions. Use the words in sentences."

Activity 278. Treasure Hunt

Take a series of photographs of various shapes and hide them in various places. Organize teams, with each team given a list of shapes to locate in a specific order. Have each team document its search in an adventure log. At the conclusion of this exercise, fill in a map indicating where they went and in what order they went there.

Activity 279. Solutions and Problems

Distribute a series of images that are solutions to problems. Have students analyze the photographs, decide what the problem is, and then photograph that problem. Record the intellectual process that led them to their conclusion.

Activity 280. Shaping Your World

"Photograph geometric shapes or concepts in the environment: the angle of two branches in a tree, the angle of a flagpole and its shadow, the convergence of beams across a ceiling. Mount the photographs on larger sheets of paper or cardboard. Using compasses and protractors, identify the angles, and analyze them in the context of the geometric concepts that they reflect—triangles, rectangles, acute triangles, and so on."

Activity 281. Rearranging Your World

Have students photograph various aspects of a chosen environment (school, neighborhood, home). The teacher then creates multiple copies of these images on a photocopy machine. Cut out these copies for students to use as building blocks with which to create entirely new environments.

Activity 282. Photo-Sculpture

"Take a series of related photographs. Create a three-dimensional wire frame consistent with theme; mount the photographs on the frame, creating a photo-sculpture. The wire frame might be spherical, for example. An alternative is to attach photos to the backs of other photographs and use them to create mobiles."

Activity 283. What's Wrong With This Picture?

"Photograph examples of incongruence in the environment, either natural or created (a tree sprouting through concrete, a sun shower, a radio in the bathtub). Describe the incongruence and specify how it might be made congruent."

Activity 284. The Built Environment

Brainstorm with students about things a shelter for people has to have (roof, roof support, door, walls, and so on). "Find and photograph examples. Look in the library or online for pictures of shelters that do not have these things." Discuss elements that are practical but not essential. "Find and photograph those elements. Finally, discuss and photograph features that are decorative. Might decorative features be important to us in some special way? Use the images to write about the built environment."

Activity 285. The Music of the Spheres

"Make images of elements in the environment that reflect the concepts of harmony and dissonance. Are these objects in harmony with one another? With their environment? Give specific examples supporting your answers."

Activity 286. Before, During, and After

"Make three photographs showing the state before a sound is created, while the sound is being created, and after the sound is completed."

Activity 287. What Makes Music *Music*?

"Photograph different objects that make sounds and place them on a linear graph covering the range from discordant noise to harmonious music."

Activity 288. A Visual Composition

"Photograph several objects." Ask students to attach a sound to the objects they photographed. "What might it sound like if it could make a sound?" Form small groups; each group should produce sound pieces by working with repetition and variation of the sounds they have created. Create a score by reducing the images and making multiple copies.

Activity 289. Goofus and Gallant

"Make images capturing appropriate and inappropriate interactions." Photographers must discuss and support their images with explanations as to what makes a particular interaction appropriate in one situation but not in another.

Activity 290. If You Can't Say Something Nice . . .

"Make images of one another. Mount each photograph on a piece of cardboard and pass it around. Write captions, which must be positive expressions about the person in the image." Mount the photos on a bulletin board. When the display is taken down, place the photo and comments in the student's portfolio.

Activity 291. Photo-Graphs

"Photograph all the people with whom you interact over a certain period (such as one day, one week, one year). Place an image of yourself at the center with the photos of others surrounding you. Draw lines from the image of you to photographs of everyone else with an explanation of who the other person is and how they interact with you."

Activity 292. My Family and Me

Ask students to photograph their family or an individual family member and describe who they are and what their relationship is with the student.

Activity 293. Daydreams

"Create a series of photographs describing individual feelings, ideas, and fantasies. Write an accompanying story that engages these self-concepts in a fantasy setting."

Activity 294. Who Am I?

"Create a series of images that describe who you are in your environment (for instance, a child in a neighborhood, the captain of the soccer team, son, daughter, cousin, nephew, or niece). Write an autobiography to accompany these photographs."

Activity 295. This Is Your Life

"Collect a series of photographs from your life (baby pictures through the present). Describe who you are in each image and how you have changed from one photograph to the next."

Activity 296. Feelings

Ask students to monitor their feelings over a period, perhaps in a "feelings journal." "Create drawings or photographs that represent those feelings." Have students present their artwork and describe what they were feeling at the time.

Activity 297. Crystal Ball

"Create an image of the future. Where will you be, what will you be doing, what circumstance brought you to this point, what decisions did you make to get here? Imagine positive and negative futures and compare them." Ask what the students can do to avoid a negative future.

Activity 298. The Dancer and the Dance

Invent a dance and photograph the sequencing of the steps involved. Tie in activities from the world of music by creating a soundtrack to accompany the dance.

Portfolios

Activity 299. The Emotional Body

Photograph the body in positions that express specific emotions. Create more of a challenge by having students wear different neutral face-masks so as not to rely on just facial expressions. Discuss how changing different aspects of those positions can change the emotion expressed.

Activity 300. The Sporting Image

"Photograph players during a sporting event. Write about the event and about what was felt and experienced, both physically and emotionally, at the moment the image was captured."

Activity 301. Body Poems

Take a simple poem or haiku and assign it to a team. Have each team come up with a physical action or gesture to stand for one line of the poem. These can be performed by individuals or as group gestures. Have all the groups perform their body poems. Document the gestures with photographs and display them with the appropriate line in the poem.

Activity 302. Living Statues

Ask students to become living statues individually or in groups to represent abstract concepts such as love, freedom, generosity, and kindness. Photograph and discuss how the students choose to represent those ideas.

Activity 303. Portfolio Ownership

Set aside an hour one day a week for students to share their photos and stories with others in the class. Ask students to create photo storybooks from their portfolios. These can be displayed in class or elsewhere in the school. Encourage collaborative projects. Students can create picture bulletin boards, collages, or mobiles that display their lives in pictures. Have them compare an old photo with a current photo. Ask them to use the photos to discuss how they are different.

Activity 304. Making Better Images

"Once you decide what the subject of your photograph is to be, move in close enough so that the subject fills the viewfinder. The result will be a more active and dramatic photograph. Be aware of the background in your image. Try to keep it as simple as possible by changing your point of view or reposing your subject. Photographs with clear subjects that make the best use of available picture space and have backgrounds free of distractions communicate more clearly."

Activity 305. Becoming Visually Literate

Select a fairly busy image. Have students sit in a circle. Pass the selected photograph around the circle and ask each student to identify one thing he or she sees in the photograph that has not been mentioned previously. Students may amplify information but must do more than simply restate something that has already been noted. This activity requires students to look deeply at an image and to listen carefully to what other students are saying.

Activity 306. Tracking Progress

Use photographs to document significant changes in the life of a student—graduation, completion of special programs, awards, and honors. Consider setting up your own merit badge program. Establish criteria and photograph students as they achieve the criteria. Make sure that your criteria reflect a full range of potential intelligences.

Activity 307. Goal Setting

Have students create an image that illustrates a personal goal. Scan the image into a computer and write information based on the following prompts:

1. "My Goal (describe in detail what you want to accomplish)."

2. "My Focus Goal (write your 'My Goal' in one sentence)."

3. "List three obstacles that might keep you from reaching your goal."

Life Skills

4. "Identify three people you could turn to for help in reaching your goal."

5. "List three things you need to learn or be able to do in order to reach your goal."

6. "List three good things that might come from reaching your goal."

7. "List eight specific objectives you will need to accomplish in order to reach your goal."

Activity 308. Learning to Learn

Devote a bulletin board to monitoring student progress. Set benchmarks and break down complex tasks into small manageable steps. Photograph students individually and install the images at the base of the bulletin board. Document progress through the skill levels by moving the images up the bulletin board. Encourage students to think of this as a team event (everyone must succeed for the team to succeed). Ask the fastest climbers if they can think of ways to help the slower climbers.

Activity 309. Project Processing

Have students scan an image into a computer that documents a completed project. They should then write the information based on the following prompts:

1. "Describe the assignment for this project."

2. "How good a job did I do on this project?"

3. "Did I get the grade I deserved? Why do I think so?"

4. "What three things could I have done to improve this project?"

Activity 310. Stories

Thinking of their image as a story might help students communicate more clearly. Just as they would do if they were writing or telling a story, have them consider the following elements when making a photograph: setting ("Where will you take the photo?"), characters ("Who will be in your photo?"), devices ("What objects will you want to include in your image?"), and drama ("What moment of action will you capture in your photograph?").

Activity 311. Teaching Tolerance

Have students interview one another with special emphasis on finding unique or unusual gifts. After an interview, students involved should make images of each other reflecting these unique talents and qualities. Post the photographs and interview notes.

Activity 312. Team Building

As an introductory assignment, challenge newly formed cooperative learning teams to create unique team pictures—the more imaginative the better. Agree to photograph the teams any way they decide. This is a fun way for new team members to form bonds of camaraderie.

Activity 313. Understanding Conflict

Analysis of conflict usually reveals a series of steps or pivotal moments at which certain options for resolution appear to fall away. Have students imagine the subtle steps in a theoretical conflict or track the stages in an actual conflict. Translate each of these steps into an image and create a display that examines the structure of the conflict.

Activity 314. Listening and Speaking From the Heart

Explain to students that a talking stick is a Native American tradition used to encourage people to listen to each other. When a group sits down in council, the talking stick is passed from person to person. Only the person holding the talking stick may speak and that person must speak briefly and honestly—from the heart. Everyone else listens deeply to what is being expressed. Ask students if they are willing to commit to using a talking stick. If so, photograph each student. Photocopy the images and cut out the face of each student. Using glue, attach the faces to a short (eighteen-inch), one-inch thick dowel rod to serve as the talking stick.

Activity 315. Calming Moment

Mount a photo of a student in the center of a paper. Ask that student to write responses to the following prompts:

1. "A person who makes me feel good about myself is . . ."

2. "A place that makes me feel safe and happy is . . ."

Life Skills

3. "A thing that I really like is . . ."

4. "Something that makes me really happy is . . ."

Activity 316. The Hero's Choice

Mount a photo of a student in the center of a paper. Ask that student to write responses to the following prompts: "Here's an example of how I . . . "

1. " . . . give in, but complain about it."

2. " . . . run away or avoid problems."

3. " . . . give in with compassion."

4. " . . . fight back and resist."

5. " . . . see the other's point of view."

6. " . . . help others see a wiser choice or course of action."

7. " . . . change the nature of the conflict so that both sides win."

8. " . . . do something surprising or funny."

Activity 317. Another Way of Seeing

Students should make two or three images that are visual metaphors for their own personality, beliefs, attitudes, likes or dislikes, hobbies, and character. The images should not have people in them. After making the photographs, ask students to explain their choices in writing or in group discussion.

Activity 318. Seeing a Future

Make a photograph of each student. Ask students to cut pictures from magazines that show people in different careers, jobs, or possible futures. Ask them to find an example of a dream job, a good job, and the worst job they could imagine. Cut the faces out of the magazine pictures and combine with the images of students so that their faces end up on the bodies of the people in the magazine images. Discuss how one might make a dream job come true or avoid ending up with the worst job they can imagine.

Activity 319. What We Might Be

Make a list of questions designed to stimulate reflection: "If you were a color, what color would you be?" Ask students to find a quiet spot and write their answers as you read about thirty questions aloud. Afterward, ask students to circle their ten most interesting or important answers. Have them write these answers on a separate sheet of paper, then add connecting words, prefixes, or suffixes as necessary. "Title the poem 'I Am!' Make a photograph that represents the poem."

Activity 320. Honoring Others

Begin with a collection of photographs depicting each student in class. Cover a bulletin board with two layers of contrasting colored paper. Trace squares the size of photographs all over the top layer, cut out three sides of each square, and fold back to make doors. On each door, identify a gift such as speaks the truth, shares freely, is a good friend, laughs often, listens well, tells good stories, finds lost things, runs fast, and so on. There should be more than enough gifts for every student in class. Then glue each student's photo behind the appropriate door.

Activity 321. Visual Connections

Each student should make one photograph. Have them examine one another's images and look for similarities. "Link images in a chain based on a common theme. See how long you can make the chain. Write descriptions or a story using the chain as an illustration."

Activity 322. Who I Am

Students should begin by listing the things that best describe them in a series of simple sentences, such as "I work well with others and am a good team member." They should write these descriptive sentences below their photograph.

Activity 323. My Owner's Manual

Mount a photo of a student in the center of a paper. Ask that student to complete the following sentences:

1. "If you want to show me you respect me . . ."

2. "If you want to show me you like me . . ."

3. "If you want to teach me something . . ."

4. "If you want to communicate with me . . ."

5. "If you want to ask me to do something . . ."

6. "If you want to help me . . ."

7. "If you want to correct me . . ."

8. "If you want to make me feel really good about myself . . ."

Activity 324. Code of Honor

Begin by soliciting input from the class regarding the qualities students most admire. These can be listed on the chalkboard and discussed. Teachers should volunteer the qualities they most admire as well, but be careful not to use this input simply for promoting classroom rules. Photograph each student for his or her individual codes of honor. In the spaces around the photo, have students draw pictures to represent the five qualities they are going to aspire to in their lives.

Activity 325. Finding Families

Begin by drawing big trees on white poster board. Ask students to bring in photocopies of as many relatives as possible that are part of their genealogy. Place an image of the student at the top of the tree with images of the parents below, then grandparents, and so on. Be sure to include guardians, adopted families, or foster families.

Activity 326. Word Connections

With students sitting in a circle, distribute to each a different and unrelated photograph. Ask the first student to stand and begin a story based on his or her image. After about thirty seconds, ring a bell to signal that the student should stop and be seated. Then ask the next students to stand and continue the story by weaving his or her image into the growing story.

Activity 327. Imagining Relationships

Allow students working in teams to select two photographs from a facedown pile of random and unrelated images. Start a five-minute timer, then have each student name some inventions suggested by the relationship of the objects in the two photos; a team recorder should write down all the inventions. The more inventions noted the better. Have the teams share their results with the class.

Life Skills

Activity 328. Photographic Documentation

Categories of photographic documentation include the following:

1. Projects: Photos of science fair projects, inventions, models, dioramas, and constructions show students as potential problem solvers.

2. Artwork: Photos of paintings, drawings, sculpture, crafts, and multimedia productions show students as creative thinkers.

3. Performances: Photos of students acting, singing, dancing, and performing instrumental music show them as being action oriented.

4. Presentations: Photos of students debating, doing oral presentations, or participating in panel discussions show them as communicators.

5. Athletics: Photos of students participating in sports show that they are well rounded, motivated, and capable of being a team player.

6. Social and extracurricular activities: Photos of students participating in community and after-school events show them as socially active, with a high level of commitment and good social skills.

Life Skills

ENHANCING SELF-ESTEEM

Activity 329. Thanks for Being Here

Take a photograph of each student as each enters the classroom. Display the photographs on a bulletin board. Have students write about themselves; display each autobiography alongside their photographs.

Activity 330. Look Who Dropped In!

Cut out colored paper shapes (such as balloons, stars, rockets, and animals). Cut a square slightly smaller than student photographs out of the center of each shape and tape student photographs to the back. This creates an instant frame and a visually exciting bulletin board. Students might list their favorite things on the colored paper for easy art photo-bios.

Activity 331. Look Who's Here

Create a rack or board with hooks or spaces for photographs of each student. Tell the students that it is their job first thing each morning to check in by placing his or her image in the appropriate space.

Activity 332. The Perfect Fit

Cover a bulletin board with paper, attach photos of your students, then cut it into irregular puzzle shapes. As a game, ask students to put the puzzle together on the board.

Activity 333. The New Student Review

Take photographs of all new students and display them on a bulletin board near the principal's office. Include an interview sheet that highlights each student's interests.

Activity 334. Meet Your Teachers

Create a bulletin board to introduce faculty to new students. Display the images of faculty members in the front lobby with their names and the subjects or grades they teach. Photograph teachers while they are active in their individual classrooms.

Activity 335. Teacher Mix-Up

Photograph every teacher from the knees down. Number the photos and have a contest to see who can identify teachers by their feet. Photograph each teacher from the top of the head to the waist, then from the waist to the feet. Mix the images to create fun photos.

Activity 336. A Birthday Timeline

Create a long paper timeline to run around your classroom (try using adding machine tape). Mark it off by days and months for one year. Place photographs of students next to their birthdays on the timeline. Create a colorful, two-dimensional party hat, and place it over a student's photograph on that student's birthday. Make sure you pick a day to celebrate summer birthdays, as well.

Activity 337. What a Year!

Using large pieces of heavy paper or cardboard to represent each month of the school year, mount photographs of all your class activities: first day of school, parents' days, special projects, field trips, holidays, the one hundredth day of school, and so on. Have students add captions to all the images. Make sure that every student is represented on the display. After displaying the calendar, bind the pages together into a scrapbook.

Activity 338. Hello, Goodbye

Collect images of students, classroom activities, visitors, special projects, field trips, and holidays and post them on a "Hello" bulletin board to greet new students the first two weeks of the following school year to show the exciting things they can look forward to doing throughout the year. Use the same display as a "Goodbye" bulletin board the final two weeks of the school year.

Activity 339. Marvelous Me Museum

Each week have a different student bring pictures from home for a class bulletin board. The pictures can be of them, their family members, where they live, and so on. They can also bring in a favorite book, or hobby, or collection to display with their photos.

Activity 340. This Is My Family

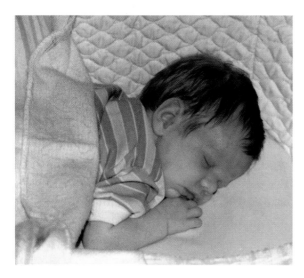

Have students glue a photograph of themselves onto a large piece of drawing paper. Ask them to draw their family members around their image. They can make it a portrait, or a picture of the family engaged in an activity they enjoy as a family.

Activity 341. Personal Profiles

Select students randomly and have them fill out a profile sheet. Take an image of each selected student and display it with the profiles in the school lobby or other special place. At the end of the display period, move the profile to the student's portfolio.

Activity 342. Shine Time

Recognize students who have shown improvement in social skills or academic areas by taking photographs of each to be displayed on a special bulletin board outside the principal's office. Give each of these "improving" students a certificate and a letter to share with parents of the "Shine Time" honor. This can be a good classroom motivator.

Activity 343. Lunch With the Principal

Each week select one student per class as "Student of the Week." Students are selected for demonstrating positive actions in work and social areas. The selected students eat lunch with the principal at a special table. Document the event with photographs.

Activity 344. Academic Superstars

Once a week, have each teacher nominate a student as an "Academic Superstar." This can be based on continued excellence, dramatic improvement, or significant effort. Recognize students who manage to get their homework in for the first time as well as straight-A students. Display photographs of the school's Academic Superstars.

Activity 345. Our Best Citizens

Each month, each teacher nominates three students for recognition as good citizens. Take photographs at an awards ceremony honoring these students and create an ongoing "Our Best Citizens" bulletin board.

Activity 346. People We Like to Have Around

Entitle a bulletin board "People We Like to Have Around Because . . . " Have students nominate their classmates for this board. To nominate a student, classmates have to complete the bulletin board title sentence orally or in writing. An example might be, "I like to have Billy around because if I lose something I know he will help me look for it."

Activity 347. The Power of Positive Students

Start a bulletin board for POPS (Power of Positive Students). Feature photographs of students who have accepted leadership roles in the school. Roles might include class officer, student council member, safety patrol, or student aid. POPS provides recognition for students and motivates them to achieve the honor of being selected.

Activity 348. Caught You Being Good

After you have clearly explained your expectations, use a camera randomly to document students meeting those expectations. Display the images on a "Caught You Being Good" bulletin board so the student receives immediate positive reinforcement.

Activity 349. Photo Awards

Create custom award certificates with a designated area for a photograph. Award the certificate along with a letter of recognition to take home and give to the parents.

Activity 350. Reading Awards

Take a photograph of each student reading a story or a favorite book; display the images on a "Reading Awards" bulletin board. This is a great incentive program to encourage students to read more. It is also a simple motivating idea for remedial reading classes or after-school and summer programs.

Enhancing Self-Esteem

Activity 351. A Special Helper

Each week, select a different student to be a special helper for the week. Have the student sit at a special desk with a special helper name placard. Create a small display board with a list of typical job duties. Photograph the special helper at work and post these images next to the display.

Activity 352. Wanted!

Create a "Wanted" poster with spaces for personal information (have fun with blank spaces for aliases). Have students fill out their "Wanted" posters with phrases like "Wanted for great schoolwork," Wanted for good attendance," "Wanted for awesome listening skills," "Wanted for shiny hair". Make sure they do not add their names. Put the posters on the bulletin board. Photograph each student and pass the pictures around the class. Students should try to match the image they have to the appropriate poster.

Activity 353. Class Critique

While evaluating students' projects in class, have them take photographs of their own work. Post the images on a bulletin board. Provide a supply of 3" × 5" cards imprinted with the words, "I like this project because . . . " and "I think this project could have been better if . . . " Have each student finish these sentences for each project on the board. Post the statements around the project photographs. Conduct a class discussion based on the display.

Activity 354. We've Got You Covered!

Cut out a magazine title or logo and glue it on white paper; make photocopies of this arrangement. Take photographs to assist students with drawing their self-portraits onto these formats. Help them imagine themselves as being worthy to be on different covers (for example, *Time*'s Student of the Year).

Activity 355. Meet the Expert

At the beginning of each week, select a student who will sit in the "Expert's" chair on Friday. Help select a student who knows a lot about a certain topic, such as football, video games, pets, games, cars, or music. Encourage the Expert to make images of the subject and to bring in samples.

On Friday, that student sits in the Expert's chair and answers questions from other students on the area of expertise. Photograph the student in the Expert's chair and use the image for a growing display on the bulletin board.

Activity 356. Interviews

Have older students interview younger students, and have them turn the interviews into articles for a school newspaper or newsletter. Add photographs of all the students involved in the project. This activity can also be done within a single classroom by having students interview their classmates about their future plans and goals.

Activity 357. Good Thoughts

Select a student each week and photograph him or her. Mount the images on sheets of letter-sized paper. Have classmates write positive messages about the student. Post the messages and photographs on the bulletin board. At the end of each week, remove the photos and pages and staple them or bind them into books. These "Good Thoughts" books can go home to share with family or be placed in student portfolios.

Activity 358. Don't Be a Turkey Day

Have students choose two or three things for which they are thankful. Have them make images to represent those things. Post these images on a Thankful Things bulletin board to serve as a daily reminder.

Activity 359. The Hall of Great Goals

Begin with a collection of photographs of each student. Cover a bulletin board with two contrasting colors of paper. Trace photograph-size squares all over the top layer of paper and cut away three sides, folding them back to form doors. On each door write a goal. These can be both short-term and long-term goals (for instance, master multiplication tables, get 100 percent correct on this week's spelling exam, and so on).

Enhancing Self-Esteem

Activity 360. Every Day's a Holiday

There are many events throughout the school year worthy of celebration. Encourage students to invent their own holiday to celebrate something or someone important to them. "When would it be? How would it be celebrated? What would it celebrate? Make a photograph to represent the new holiday." Post the new holidays on a calendar and celebrate them during the year.

Activity 361. Masks

Have students photograph one another expressing an attitude or feeling by making their faces into masks. "Make a chart. On one side write a brief description of a mask and the feeling it represents. Next to it describe what the mask wearer might have been feeling at the time. Finally, match the photos with the true descriptions."

Activity 362. Reflection—Projection

Have students choose an important life event from the past year. "Make a photograph that represents that event. Label the image 'reflection.'" Then ask students to select personal goals for the coming year. "Make a photograph that represents that goal. Label that image 'projection.'" Include the photographs along with written explanations of them in student portfolios.

Activity 363. Gift Catalogue

Have students make a list of things that can be enjoyed for free. Photograph those things and place them in a "priceless" catalogue.

Activity 364. Me, Myself, and I

Have each student pair with a classmate to take photographs of each other. They should write about how they look in their photos. Photographs brought from home can be added to create visual history. Finally, each student should write an autobiography using the supporting images and interview text. The same procedure can be used to create biographies of others outside the classroom.

Activity 365. Photo Hall Passes

Create unique hall passes by selecting an object that is fun and easy to carry. Attach a clear vinyl pocket to the object. Photograph places in the school such as office, restroom, library, media center, nurse's office, cafeteria, and gym. When students use the hall pass, insert the destination photo in the holder.

Activity 366. Conflict Resolution

Photograph examples of desirable and undesirable behavior. Discuss why these behaviors are desirable and undesirable. Using the photographs of behaviors, make a wall chart that can be referred to daily. Highlight positive choices in resolving conflicts. Emphasize teamwork and getting along with others. Stop conflicts by having everyone freeze. Have a disinterested party summarize the conflict as he or she sees it and suggest a positive course of action.

Activity 367. Fame

Take a photo of each student, or allow him or her to photograph another student so that the photo can be used for an advertisement for that person. "Choose a famous person you admire. Why is that person famous? Using your photo, list why you, too, could be famous." Post these photos around the room.

Activity 368. Bringing Cheer

Use photos of the class on cards sent to students who are ill. Photograph students doing activities around the class in groups and encourage them to personalize the images with their own sentiments.

Activity 369. Class Books

During special events, snap enough photos to ensure that every student appears in at least one photo. Mount the images on individual pages and encourage each student to fill in and decorate the rest of the page that has their photo. Have them write about what they liked best about the event. Compile these in a three-ring binder. At the end of the year, give each student a photocopy of all the pages in the binder.

Activity 370. Teamwork

Assign students to cooperative learning teams and make a team photo. Ask them to do something representational and creative. Mount the photos on poster board and have the team keep track of their individual and group success on the poster.

Activity 371. People You Should Know

Create a bulletin board of people in the school that students should know such as the librarian, nurse, principal, assistant principal, cafeteria worker, and custodian. Photograph these people and keep them posted on a bulletin board where students can identify them.

Activity 372. Bus Books

For bus drivers at a school with a PreK busing program, compile a notebook of student photographs with names, addresses, bus stop location, and phone numbers. This helps ensure students are on the right bus. It is especially valuable to substitute drivers.

Activity 373. Parent/Guardian Photos

For younger students, try to get a photo of each student's parent or guardian at preschool registration. Punch holes in the top and thread string through the photo so that students can wear a familiar photo for the first couple of days of school. After that, mount the photos on a bulletin board.

Activity 374. A Day in the Life

Allow students to check out a camera for a day and create "A Day in the Life" photo essay about how they spend their day. Have students create a photo essay in book or poster form and present it to the class.

Activity 375. Photo Cubes

Cut out squares of cardboard large enough for photographs. Tape them together to form cubes. On the top of each cube have a student list his or her strengths. On the bottom of the cube have them list their weaknesses. On the four remaining sides have them create four photographs or a combination of images and drawings that represent four aspects of their personality.

Activity 376. Group Shot

Whenever you have a special event or field trip, commemorate it with a group photo. Have copies made for each student in class. Have students put the images in their class journals.

Activity 377. First Day of School Premiere

On the first day of school, have teachers meet the buses to photograph groups of students arriving at school. Play fanfare music on the loud speaker. Treat them like movie stars. Place all the photographs on a lobby bulletin board.

GLOBAL HOLIDAYS

January

New Year's Day (International)

Epiphany, 3 Kings Day (Christian)

Martin Luther King Jr. Day (U.S.)

Hajj (Islamic)

February

Candlemas (Christian)

Nirvana Day (Buddhist)

Shrove Tuesday (Christian)

Black History Month (U.S.)

Maha Shivaratri (Hindu)

Chinese New Year (China)

Vietnamese New Year/Tet (Vietnam)

Ash Wednesday (Christian)

Lent Begins (Christian)

Hijra/New Year (Islamic)

Vasant Panchami (Hindu)

Valentine's Day (International)

Ashura (Islamic)

President's Day (U.S.)

Holi (Hindu)

March

St. Patrick's Day (Christian)

Palm Sunday (Christian)

Spring Equinox (International)

Norooz/The New Day (Zoroastrian)

Naw-Ruz/New Year's Day (Bahá'í)

Maundy Thursday (Christian)

Purim (Jewish)

Good Friday (Christian)

Magha Puja Day (Buddhist)

Easter (Christian)

April

April Fool's Day (International)

Ramayana (Hindu)

Baisakhi (Sikh)

Ramanavami (Hindu)

Mawlid an Nabi (Islamic)

Earth Day (International)

Pesach/Passover (Jewish)

May

May Day (U.S./Europe)

Cinco de Mayo (Mexico)

Mother's Day (International)

Yom Hasho'ah (Jewish)

Pentecost (Christian)

Declaration of the Báb (Bahá'í)

Buddha Day/ Visakha Puja (Buddhist)

Memorial Day (U.S.)

Arbor Day (U.S.)

June

Shavuot (Jewish)

Flag Day (U.S.)

Father's Day (International)

Summer Solstice (International)

First Nation's Day (Canadian Native People)

July

Independence Day (U.S.)

Martyrdom of the Báb (Bahá'í)

Ulambana/Obon (Buddhist)

Bastille Day (France)

Asalha Puja Day (Hindu)

Pioneer Day (Mormon Christian)

August

Tisha B'av (Jewish)

Raksha Bandhan (Hindu)

Krishan Jayanti (Hindu)

September

Lailet al Miraj (Islamic)

Labor Day (U.S.)

Native American Day (U.S.)

Ganesh Chaturthi (Hindu)

Lailat al Bara'ah (Islamic)

Fall Equinox (International)

October

Ramadan Begins (Islamic)

Rosh Hashanah (Jewish)

Navaratra Dashara (Hindu)

Columbus Day (U.S.)

Día de la Raza (Latin America)

Dasera (Hindu)

Yom Kippur (Jewish)

Sukkot (Jewish)

Birth of the Báb (Bahá'í)

Guru Tegh Bahadur

Martyrdom (Sikh)

Quds Day (Islamic)

Halloween (U.S.)

November

Día de los Muertos (Mexico)

All Saints' Day (Christian)

Diwali (Hindu)

Id al-Fitr/ Ramadan Ends (Islamic)

Election Day (U.S.)

Veterans Day (U.S.)

Birth of Bahá u'lláh (Bahá'í)

Thanksgiving (U.S.)

First Sunday of Advent (Christian)

December

Bodhi Day/Rohatsu (Buddhist)

Our Lady of Guadalupe Feast Day (Catholic Christian)

Global Holidays

December (Continued)

Winter Solstice (International)	Kwanza (U.S.)	New Year's Eve (International)
Christmas (Christian)	Hanukkah (Jewish)	

Activity 378. Happy New Year!

Discuss some of the major events that happened in the world during the past year. Discuss local events and class events as well. Ask students to make metaphorical photographs of how they view the upcoming year.

Activity 379. Make Dreams Come True

Discuss with the class what can be done to make dreams come true. Ask the class to identify a dream that they could collectively realize. This could become a class project that provides a multidisciplinary focus for their studies. Document the various stages of the project with photographs.

Activity 380. African American Heroes

Historical heroes should be recognized for their achievements throughout the year. Ethnicity is cultural history. Discuss the many important figures in our nation's history and their contributions to progress. Each student should select a local African American official, politician, policeperson, doctor, or judge, then photograph and interview them about their contributions to the community.

Activity 381. I Love Me, I Love Me Not, I Love Me!

Have students create lists of the things they love about themselves. Students should use words and images to express their great qualities. Make a Valentine with one of the photos from each student to themselves.

Activity 382. If I Were President . . .

Have the students imagine the perfect nation. Discuss what it might look like and how it would differ from the nation as we know it. Make photographs illustrating this vision and mount them on pages in the form of a picture book with descriptive captions. Lead a discussion on the responsibilities of leadership and explore the reality of transforming visions into actions.

Global Holidays

Activity 383. Good Luck!

A four-leaf clover is a symbol of good luck. Have students create their own photographic symbols of good luck. "Imagine and create the history behind the symbol. Write a legend that reveals how the symbol became associated with luck. Mount the photograph on the document."

Activity 384. Religious Culture

Discuss the importance of religion in history. Try to brainstorm as many different religious cultures as possible. Make photographs of different places of worship in the local community.

Activity 385. Not!

Things are not always as they seem. Each student should make some photographic illusions or visual trickery. Lead a discussion about impressions: first/lasting, honest/false. Students should begin a collection of images that cause misconceptions. "Describe how the message in the image is misleading and its potential to lead to misinterpretation. Make a partner photograph that provides a clear and concise interpretation, thereby diminishing the visual trickery."

Activity 386. On Earth

Have students discuss the importance of caring for our planet. Have them photograph examples of litter and air pollution. They can then write what needs to be changed in each image in order to ensure a cleaner, better planet.

Activity 387. A New Beginning

Springtime is a season of starting anew: new growth, new hope, and new opportunity. Ask students to make a photograph representing something about themselves that they would like to change. The key is to avoid being literal. The student is creating an image that represents a change he or she would like to undergo; there should be no pictures of people in this activity. Have students take turns explaining why they chose particular images. What is it they would like to change? Why?

Activity 388. May Day

Have students make many photographs of different types of flowers. Ask them to tape each image to a stick or twig. Place the image flowers in a basket arrangement to be displayed in the classroom. Talk about the origins of May Day, the springtime celebration of the coming of summer.

Activity 389. The Cultural Gazette

A global community represents more than just an understanding of cultural differences: it represents sharing. Have students discuss the importance of the fifth of May. Why is it a time of celebration? Celebrate the different aspects of Cinco de Mayo: clothing, dance, music, food, and traditions. Appoint students to be photojournalists for the day of events. The images can be used in a school newsletter.

Activity 390. Mother's Day

Ask students to talk about the many things they enjoy about their mothers. Make a photograph of each student and mount it on a card made from construction paper. Have students compose a poem or write their expressions of sentiment.

Activity 391. A Day to Remember

Remembering and memorializing events or people enhance the fabric of our daily lives. Each student should think of and list a few things from the past that are extremely important. Discuss or write about the reasons for these particular choices. Make photographs, either abstract or realistic, that are memorials to these things. The photos can directly relate to the memory or they can be entirely symbolic, expressing the feelings that are a part of that memory. Put up a classroom memorial wall with photos and brief captions.

Activity 392. Plant a Tree

Trees provide oxygen and homes for insects, birds, animals, and people. Discuss other uses for trees, such as building materials, paper, shade, firewood, pencils, and beauty. Photograph some of the many ways trees contribute to our world. Plant a tree on the school's property. Photograph the tree each month to document its growth.

Activity 393. Long May You Wave

Discuss the American flag, its history, and how it has changed. Discuss other country's flags and state flags. Photograph as many different flags as you can find to be placed in a "Book of Flags." Have students write about each flag, its name, origin, and symbolism.

Activity 394. Father's Day

Ask students to talk about the many things they enjoy about their fathers. Make a photograph of each student and mount it on a card made from construction paper. Have students compose a poem or write their expressions of sentiment.

Activity 395. Canada, Oh Canada

Discuss Canadian cultures and history. Talk about Canada's different climates, laws, and communities. How are those different in the United States? Photograph examples of these differences in recognition of First Nation's Day.

Activity 396. Home of the Free

Discuss the traditions cele-brated each July fourth: parades, picnics, fireworks, and so on. Have students research our country's independence and discuss how it affects our daily lives. Have students make metaphorical images of what it is like to live in a free country.

Activity 397. Bastille Day

After doing activities in celebration of Independence Day, lead a discussion about Bastille Day. Talk about the similarities between the two holidays. Make a photograph of the French flag and mount it with an essay about France's national holiday.

Activity 398. Hi Ho, Hi Ho, It's Off to Work We Go!

Students should think of two or three occupations that they would like to do. Ask them to assess a list of the good things and a list of the drawbacks for each of the occupations. Use photographs to illus-trate the lists. Reassess student choices based on objective descriptions of the positives and negatives. Finally, order the choices according to preference.

Activity 399. This Land Is Your Land, This Land Is Our Land

When we think of "Indians," what comes to mind for those of us who are not Native Americans? Have students make their own personal list of Native American characteristics. Explore the lists, discussing prejudice and stereotyping. Students should now conduct research to discover genuine Native American values and the realities of the Native American experience. Be aware that there are many different tribes, languages, religions, and customs. There are and always have been varying degrees of assimilation into "American" culture. Have the students use photos to illustrate the things that they have learned by searching for the "first" Americans, including both realities and prejudices. Look at the parallels in current and past immigration patterns of different ethnic groups.

Activity 400. Autumn's Beginning

Lead the students into a discussion about the Fall Equinox. Search the Internet to research the proximity of the sun to Earth during the period of September 20 through the 23. Have students make photographs of physical signs of the beginning of the autumn season.

Activity 401. The Age of Discovery

Every day is a unique opportunity to discover something and to learn something new. Make a "Discovery" bulletin board as an ongoing project. Have students photograph newly discovered objects and people that they did not know. Have them write down recent discoveries made in class during the multisubject lessons.

Activity 402. Disguises

Halloween is a time of playful disguise, of wearing masks and costumes to pretend to be someone other than ourselves. Have students seek out ordinary objects and photograph them in a way that would make that object unrecognizable. Encourage them to turn their cameras on different angles and to use lighting to aid in their disguise.

Activity 403. The Day of the Dead

The two most important things for students to know about the Mexican Day of the Dead (Día de los Muertos) are these:

1. It is a holiday with a complex history, and therefore its observance varies quite a bit by region and by degree of urbanization.

2. It is not a morbid but rather a festive occasion.

Discuss the Mexican holiday and have students illustrate their understanding through photographs and written reports.

Activity 404. It's About Time

Create a timeline for the school year (September to June). The timeline will be narrow (twelve inches) and long (ten to fifteen feet), and be the perfect size to run along top of the blackboard. Each time something significant happens in the classroom, have a student make a photograph for the timeline.

Activity 405. We the Students . . .

The right to vote is one of the most important elements of any democracy. Our students will determine our future. Join the students in a discussion about the election process. Set up a mock election in your classroom, focusing on real local or national candidates. Encourage students to make images that support the candidates' stands on the issues. Make posters and pamphlets. Vote!

Activity 406. We Salute You

Veterans' Day (formerly Armistice Day), November 11, is the anniversary of the Armistice, which was signed in the Compiègne Forest by the Allies and the Germans in 1918, ending World War I after four years of conflict. Lead the students in a discussion about the many people who have fought in wars throughout history and how Veterans' Day gives us the opportunity to celebrate them and their sacrifices. Have students find veterans in their community, photograph them, and conduct an interview regarding their service to their country.

Global Holidays

Activity 407. Thanks for Giving

At Thanksgiving, we pause to appreciate and give thanks for what we have. Many people in this world do not have the things we take for granted, such as clean water, food, and shelter. Start a schoolwide community campaign to collect things of need for homeless shelters in your area. Document the project with photographs and write an article for the school newsletter.

Activity 408. A Gift Isn't Always a Present

Many religious holidays include the tradition of giving gifts. It is an exercise of values and an expression of kindness, not always in the material form. Ask students to make photographs to give as gifts to people in their lives: flowers, sunshine, friendship, and so on.

Activity 409. The Winter Solstice

In the northern hemisphere, the winter solstice is the day of the year (near December 22) when the sun is farthest south. In the southern hemisphere, winter and summer solstices are exchanged so that the winter solstice is the day on which the sun is farthest north. Lead the students into a discussion about the winter solstice. "Search the Internet to research the proximity of the sun to the earth." Have students make photographs of physical signs of the beginning of the winter season.

Conclusion

ood teaching is an art. Learning styles are woven into all college methods courses. Someday—and yes, this *will* happen—a student will appear at your classroom door and say, "You've never met anyone like me before. I wasn't in your college textbooks or methods courses. I can't depend on your fancy building, materials, or curriculum. All I can do is to look to you, my teacher, and see if you have what it takes to look at me for who I am and help me to learn to the best of my ability."

Therein lies the challenge, the very reason you are reading this book. One day a student will validate your career—trust me on this one. They'll leave your classroom, but they won't go away, nor should they. Although you may find common threads, all children learn differently. Study your students. Learn their strengths and weaknesses. You need to know whom you are teaching. Remember that your students will become risk takers only after you have created a safe environment for them. Give them plenty of space to stumble, adjust, and experiment with the thinking process. Allow your passion for teaching to be blatant; no matter how proficient you are in the teaching process, your success is ultimately determined by your passion. No matter how abstract or difficult your lessons become, be clear and keep it simple. It's very easy to make material seem far more difficult than it needs to be. Don't be afraid to become vulnerable. There's nothing wrong with not having every answer to every question. In fact, it's human.

The key is to maintain a balance, and maintain credibility. If you listen to your heart, it will become the core to your teaching ability. The best blues musician pours his heart into a microphone or an amplifier. Be redundant. William H. Rastetter, who taught at MIT and Harvard, said, "The first time you say something, it's heard. The second time, it's recognized. The third time, it's learned" (Salter, 2001). Challenge your students with strong questions. Skilled debaters challenge themselves to side with either end of an issue before taking a stance. These challenges rarely come from questions that simply require a yes or no response. Lead the classroom but don't become a dictator. Teach your students how to think, and allow them to learn how to learn. You will find yourself in a much more productive role as a facilitator, as opposed to a leader. The pathway to learning runs in both directions. Teaching is talking and listening; in time, you will become skilled at what to listen for. Ninety-five percent of what a student learns, he or she has taught to someone else (Dale Cone of Experience). As a teacher, you are part of a triangle. Peer-to-peer teaching is a must. Reflect on your own school days as a young student. Remember what it was like when much of the class understood a concept and you did not. Revisit that feeling and use it to avoid using the same teaching strategy for everyone in your classroom. The quickest way to comprehension is not always a straight line. And finally, always be the switched-on teacher. Whether it is in a grocery store on a Saturday afternoon, in the school cafeteria, or in the teacher's parking lot, teaching is not just a practice of professional skills—it's a personality.

References

3M Corporation. (2001). *Polishing your presentation: 3M meeting network articles & advice.*

American Heritage Dictionary, 2nd ed. (1989). New York: Dell Publishing.

Business Editors/Education Writers. (2003). AEL and Inspiration Software announce research review supporting use of graphic organizers to improve student skills: Twenty-nine studies meeting No Child Left Behind research criteria examined by independent institute. Business Wire August 6.

Buzan, T., & Buzan, B. (1996). *The mind map book: How to use radiant thinking to maximize your brain's untapped potential.* New York: Plume Books.

Campbell, D. (1997). *The Mozart effect: Tapping the power of music to heal the body, strengthen the mind and unlock the creative spirit.* New York: William Morrow & Company.

Center for Media Literacy. (n.d.) Media literacy: A definition . . . and more. Retrieved November 18, 2008 from http://www.medialit.org/reading_room/rr2def.php.

CNN. (2003). Live from the headlines, Interview with David Walsh (May 29). Retrieved November 18, 2008 from http://transcripts.cnn.com/TRANSCRIPTS/0305/29/se.07.html.

Coe, M. D. (1992). *Breaking the Maya code.* New York: Thames and Hudson.

Davis Dyslexic Association International. (n.d.) Quotes from famous dyslexics. http://www.dyslexiacenter.org/ar/000045.shtml.

Day, M. (1997). *Kairos* 2, no. 1.

deBono, E. (1970). *Lateral thinking.* New York: Harper & Row.

Diamond, M. (1999). *The magic trees of the mind.* New York: Dutton/Plume.

Dyc, G., & Milligan, C. (2000). *Native American visual vocabulary: Ways of thinking and living.* Paper presented at the National Association of Native American Studies Section, Houston, TX, February 21–26.

Edutopia. (2004). Life on the screen: Visual literacy in education. Retrieved November 17, 2008 from http://www.edutopia.org/life-screen.

Edwards, B. (1999). *The new drawing on the right side of the brain.* Rutherford, NJ: Putnam Publishing Group.

Entertainment Software Association. (2008). Industry facts. Retrieved November 17, 2008 from http://www.theesa.com/facts/index.asp.

Ewald, W. (2002). *I wanna take me a picture.* Boston: Beacon Press.

Fadiman, C. (1985). *The Little, Brown book of anecdotes.* Boston: Little, Brown.

Fink, G. R., Marshall, J. C., Weiss, P. H., Shah, N. J., Toni, I., Halligan, P. W., et al. (2000). "Where" depends on "what": A differential functional anatomy for position discrimination in one- versus two-dimensions. *Neuropsychologia* 38, no. 13, 1741–1748.

Gallaga, O. L. (2008). Austin's Aspyr to bring SAT prep to Nintendo DS. *Austin American-Statesman*, April 15.

Gangwer, T., & Rzadko-Henry, G. (2003). *English works in America—EL Civics & ESL: Visual communication tools for teachers*. Round Rock, TX: Zena Books.

Gardner, H. (1983). *Frames of mind: The theory of multiple intelligences.* New York: BasicBooks.

Gardner, H. (1993). *Multiple intelligences: The theory in practice.* New York: BasicBooks.

Gellevij, M., Van-der-Meij, H., deJong, T., Pieters, J. (2002). Multimodal versus unimodal instruction in a complex learning context. *Journal of Experimental Education* 70, no. 3, 215–39.

Green, R., E. (1984). The persuasive properties of color. *Marketing Communications* (October).

Grunwald Associates, LLC. (2008). *Safe and smart.* Bethesda, MD.

Haggbloom, S. J., Warnick, R., Warnick, J. E., Jones, V. K., Yarbrough, G. L., Russell, T. M., et al. (2002). The 100 most eminent psychologists of the 20th century. *Review of General Psychology* 6, no. 2, 139–152.

Healy, J. (1994). *Your child's growing mind.* New York: Doubleday.

Hewlett-Packard. (1999). *Advisor* (June).

Horn, R. E. (2001). Visual language and converging technologies in the next 10–15 years and beyond. A paper for the National Science Foundation Conference on Converging Technologies, December.

Hucko, B. (1996). *A rainbow at night: The world in words and pictures by Navajo children.* San Francisco: Chronicle Books.

Hyerle, D. (2000). *A field guide to using visual tools.* Alexandria, VA: Association for Supervision and Curriculum Development.

Institute for the Advancement of Research in Education (IARE) at Appalachia Educational Laboratory/Advantia (AEL). (2003). *Graphic organizers: A review of scientifically based research.* Charleston, WV.

International Dyslexia Association (IDA). 2002. Just the facts: Definition of dyslexia. Retrieved November 17, 2008 from http://www.interdys.org/ewebeditpro5/upload/Definition_Fact_Sheet_3-10-08.pdf.

Jensen, N. (2005). Retrieved October 29, 2008 from http://www.natespace.com.

Kaiser Foundation. (2005). Media multi-tasking: Changing the amount and nature of young people's media use. Retrieved November 17, 2008 from http://www.kff.org/entmedia/entmedia030905nr.cfm.

Kohlberg, L. (1963). The development of children's orientation toward moral order: Sequence in the development of moral thought. *Vita Humana,* 6, 11–33.

Kornhaber, M. L. (2001). Howard Gardner. In J. A. Palmer (ed.) *Fifty modern thinkers on education: From Piaget to the present.* London: Routledge.

Kranzler, J. (1999). Innovator: Judy Kranzler. *Blueprint* 4 (Fall). Democratic Leadership Council, Washington, DC.

Landon, B. (2005). Douglas College Psychology Department. Retrieved November 17, 2008 from. http://eideneurolearningblog .blogspot.com/2005/02/visual-learning-style-as-kaleidoscope.html.

Levy, I., Hasson, U., & Malach, R. (2004). One picture is worth at least a million neurons. *Current Biology* (14): 996–1001.

Levy, J., Trevarthen, C. & Sperry, R. W. (1972). Perception of bilateral chimeric figures following hemispheric deconnexion. *Brain* no. 95, 61–78.

Lucas, G. (2004). Life on the screen. *Edutopia* 1, September.

Luscher, M. (1948/1969). *The Luscher color test*. New York: Random House.

Marzano, R., Pickering, D., & Pollack, J. (2001). *Classroom instruction that works*. Colorado Springs, CO: Mid-continent Research for Education and Learning (McREL).

Mind Tools Ltd. (1998). *How your learning style affects use of mnemonics*. Yapton, UK: Mind Tools.

Moreno, R., & Duran, R. (2004). Do multiple representations need explanations? The role of verbal guidance and individual differences in multimedia mathematics learning. *Journal of Educational Psychology* 96, no. 3, 492–503.

Morton, J. L. (n.d.) Color matters. Retrieved November 17, 2008 from http://www.colormatters.com/body_pink.html.

National Academy of Sciences. 2001. Proceedings of the National Academy of Sciences (September 25) 98, no. 20, 11818–11823.

National School Boards Association (NSBA). (2008). *Research & guidelines for children's use of the Internet*. Alexandria, VA: NSBA.

Olmeda, I. (2003). Language mediation among emerging bilingual children. *Linguistics and Education* 14, no. 2.

Padolsky, D. (2006.) Ask NCELA no.1: How many school-aged English-language learners (ELLs) are there in the U.S.? American Community Survey Special Calculation. Provided to the U.S. Department of Education, Office of English Language Acquisition, Washington, DC.

Pantone. (2008). How does color affect us? Retrieved November 17, 2008 from (http://www.pantone.com/pages/pantone/Pantone.aspx?pg=19382&ca=29).

Ratey, J. (2001). *A user's guide to the brain. Perception, attention and the four theaters of the brain*. Toronto, Canada: Pantheon Books.

Restak, R. (2003). *The new brain: How the modern age is rewiring your brain*. New York: Rodale Books.

Rosenberg, M. (1992). Playing chess as a tool in learning, *New York Times*, October 11.

Rzadko-Henry, G. (2005). *A moveable museum*. Clarkston, MI: Raining Butterflies Publishing.

Sadoski, M., & Paivio, A. (2002). Response. [Response to a review of the book *Imagery and text: A dual coding theory of reading and writing*]. *British Journal of Educational Psychology*, 72, 148–149.

Schaefer, J. (1995). *Sight unseen: The art of active seeing*. New York: Harper-Collins.

Shaywitz, S. (2005). *Overcoming dyslexia*. New York. Knopf Publishing Group/Random House.

Shaywitz, S. (2008). Children of the code (interview transcript). Retrieved November 17, 2008 from http://www.childrenofthecode.org/interviews/shaywitz.htm.

Sinatra, R. (1986). *Creating success in the classroom! Visual organizers and how to use them*. Springfield, IL: Charles C Thomas.

Stix, A. (1996). *The need for pictorial journal writing*. Paper presented at the Westchester Teachers' Center Conference, Math enrichment for all, Hartsdale, NY.

Swanson, H. L. Sáez, L. Gerber, M. Leafstedt, J. (2004). Literacy and cognitive functioning in bilingual and nonbilingual children at or not at risk for reading disabilities. *Journal of Educational Psychology* 96, no. 1, 3–18.

Teachers of English to Speakers of Other Languages (TESOL). (n.d.) ESL Standards for PreK–12 Students. Retrieved November 17, 2008 from http://www.tesol.org/s_tesol/seccss.asp?CID=113&DID=1583.

Walker, M. (1991). *The power of color*. Garden City Park, NY: Avery Publishing.

Wallechinsky, D., Wallace, A., Wallace, I. (1977). *The book of lists*. London, UK: Corgi Books.

Suggested Reading

Adair King, J. (2000). *Digital photography for dummies* (3rd ed.) Boston: IDG Books Worldwide.

Allen Ewy, C., & Marzano, R. J. (2002). *Teaching with visual frameworks.* Thousand Oaks, CA: Corwin Press.

Berger, J. (1995). *Ways of seeing.* London: Penguin Books.

Buckingham, D. (2003). *Media education: Literacy, learning and contemporary culture.* Cambridge, UK: Polity Press.

Burmark, L. (2004). *Visual literacy.* Alexandria, VA: Association for Supervision and Curriculum Development.

Caine, G., & Caine, R.N. (Eds.) (1994). *Making connections: Teaching and the human brain.* Menlo Park, CA: Addison-Wesley.

Campbell, D. (1983). *Introduction to the musical brain.* St. Louis, MO: Magnamusic.

Chapman, C. (1993). *If the shoe fits . . . How to develop multiple intelligences in the classroom.* Palatine, IL: IRI/Skylight Publishing.

Crockett, T. (2000). *The artist inside.* New York: Broadway Books.

Debes, J. (1969). The loom of visual literacy. *Audiovisual Instruction* 14, no. 8, 25–27.

Dunn, R., & Dunn, K. (1978). *Teaching students through their individual learning styles: A practical approach.* Englewood Cliffs, NJ: Prentice Hall.

Eiseman, L. (2000). *Pantone guide to communicating with color.* Cincinnati, OH: North Light Books.

Eliot, L. (1999). *What's going on in there? How the brain and mind develop in the first five years of life.* New York: Bantam Books.

Fei, V. L. (2006). The visual semantics stratum: making meanings in sequential images. In T. Royce & W. Bowcher (Eds.), *New directions in the analysis of multimodal discourse.* Mahwah, NJ: Lawrence Erlbaum Associates.

Feller, B. (2006). Scientists say video games can reshape education. *The Seattle Times*, October 18.

Frey, N., & Fisher, D. (Eds.). (2008). *Teaching visual literacy: Using comic books, graphic novels, anime, cartoons, and more to develop comprehension and thinking skills.* Thousand Oaks, CA: Corwin Press.

Gangwer, T. (1990). *From both sides of the desk: The best teacher I never had.* Houston, TX: Larksdale.

Grandin, T. (2006). *Thinking in pictures: and other reports from my life with autism.* New York: Doubleday, Vintage Press Division of Random House.

Greenberg, S. (1999). *The complete idiot's guide to digital photography.* Indianapolis, IN: Que Corporation.

Grinder, M. (1991). *Righting the educational conveyor belt.* Portland, OR: Metamorphous Press.

Hampden-Turner, C. (1981). *Maps of the mind.* New York: Macmillan Publishing.

Iaccino, J. (1993). *Left-brain–right-brain differences: Inquiries, evidence, and new approaches.* Hillsdale, NJ: Lawrence Erlbaum & Associates.

Impact II—The Teachers Network. (1988). *New teachers handbook* (2nd ed.). New York: Impact II.

Impact II—The Teachers Network. (1989). *Teacher/parent partnerships handbook.* New York: Impact II.

Impact II—The Teachers Network. (1991). *The teachers' vision of the future of education: A challenge to the nation.* New York: Impact II.

Jensen, E. (1996). *Brain-based learning.* Del Mar, CA: Turning Point Publishing.

Katz, L. C., & Manning, R. (1999). *Keep your brain alive.* New York: Workman Publishing.

Kaufeldt, M. (1999). *Begin with the brain: Orchestrating the learner-centered classroom.* Tucson, AZ: Zephyr Press.

Kohlberg, L., & Turiel, E. (1971). Moral development and moral education. In G. Lesser, ed., *Psychology and educational practice.* Glenview, IL: Scott Foresman.

Kohlberg, L., Lickona, T., (Eds.) (1976). *Moral stages and moralization: The cognitive-developmental approach, moral development and behavior: Theory, research and social issues.* Austin, TX: Rinehart and Winston.

Kovalik, S. (2001). *Exceeding expectations: A user's guide to implementing brain research in the classroom.* Covington, WA: Books for Educators.

Kreger Silverman, L. (2002). *Upside-down brilliance: The visual-spatial learner.* Denver, CO: DeLeon Publishing.

Lazear, D. (1991). *Seven ways of teaching: The artistry of teaching with multiple intelligences.* Palatine, IL: IRI/Skylight Publishing.

Margulies, N. (1991). *Mapping inner space.* Tucson, AZ: Zephyr Press.

Marzano, R. (1992). *A different kind of classroom.* Alexandria, VA: Association for Supervision and Curriculum Development.

Milbrath, C., and Siegol, B. (1996). *Perspective taking in the drawings of a talented autistic child.* Visual Arts Research, School of Arts and Design, University of Illinois, Urbana, IL, 56–75.

Moline, S. (1995). *I see what you mean: Children at work with visual information.* York, ME: Stenhouse Publishers.

Moseley, N. (2002). Italia Conti Academy of Theatre Arts. Sanford Meisner. *The Literary Encyclopedia.* http://www.litencyc.com/.

Paivio, A. (1971). *Imagery and verbal processes.* New York: Holt, Reinhart, and Winston.

Piaget, J. (1932). *The moral judgment of the child.* London: Kegan Paul, Trench, Trubner and Co.

Pink, D. H. (2005). *A whole new mind: Moving from the information age to the conceptual age.* New York: Penguin Group.

Reilly, B. (1997). *Create PowerPoint presentations in a weekend.* Rocklin, CA: Prima Publishing.

Salter, C. (2001). Attention, class!! 16 ways to be a smarter teacher. *Fast Company* (53). Fast Company, New York.

Seirawan, Y. (1994). Scholastic chess: Feel the buzz? *Inside Chess* 5, no. 4, 3–4.

Shibukawa, I. (1991). *Designer's guide to color 5.* San Francisco: Chronicle Books.

Smith, A. (1998). *Accelerated learning in practice: Brain-based methods for accelerating motivation and achievement.* Bristol, UK: Network Educational Press.

Smith, M. K. (2002). Howard Gardner and multiple intelligences. The encyclopedia of informal education, London. http://www.infed.org/thinkers/gardner.htm.

Sousa, D. A. (2005). *How the brain learns,* 3rd ed. Thousand Oaks, CA: Corwin Press.

Sylwester, R. (2000). *Biological brain in a cultural classroom.* London, UK: Corwin Press.

West, T. G. (1991). *In the mind's eye.* Buffalo, NY: Prometheus.

Wolfe, P. (2001). *Brain matters: Translating research into classroom practice.* Alexandria, VA: Association for Supervision and Curriculum Development.

Index

CORWIN PRESS

The Corwin Press logo—a raven striding across an open book—represents the union of courage and learning. Corwin Press is committed to improving education for all learners by publishing books and other professional development resources for those serving the field of PreK–12 education. By providing practical, hands-on materials, Corwin Press continues to carry out the promise of its motto: **"Helping Educators Do Their Work Better."**